# The
# Czech
# Americans

THE IMMIGRANT EXPERIENCE

# The Czech Americans

Stephanie Sakson-Ford

CHELSEA HOUSE PUBLISHERS

Philadelphia

**CHELSEA HOUSE PUBLISHERS**
Editor-in-Chief: Stephen Reginald
Production Manager: Pamela Loos
Art Director: Sara Davis
Picture Editor: Judy Hasday
Senior Production Editor: Lisa Chippendale

**Staff for THE CZECH AMERICANS**
Contributing Author: Derek Davis
Production Editor: Debby Stuart
Cover Illustrator: Jane Sterrett

First Printing
1   3   5   7   9   8   6   4   2

**Library of Congress Cataloging-in-Publication Data**
Sakson-Ford, Stephanie.
   The Czech Americans / Stephanie Sakson-Ford.
      p.   cm. — (Immigrant experience)
   Includes bibliographical references (p.    ) and index.
   ISBN 0-7910-5052-1.
         0-7910-5054-8 (pbk.)
   1. Czech Americans—Juvenile literature.   I. Title.   II. Series.
E184.B67S23   1998
973'.049186—dc21                                                    98-19608
                                                                          CIP
                                                                          AC

# CONTENTS

Introduction: "A Nation of Nations"  7

A New Beginning  13

A Proud History  17

The Earliest Arrivals  39

A Wave of Immigration  47

Where City and Country Meet  61

Picture Essay: Moving Ahead, Looking Back  65

Religion and Community  85

An Era of Excellence  97

Further Reading  108

Index  109

# THE IMMIGRANT EXPERIENCE

A LAND OF IMMIGRANTS

THE AFRICAN AMERICANS

THE AMERICAN INDIANS

THE AMISH

THE ARAB AMERICANS

THE CHINESE AMERICANS

THE CUBAN AMERICANS

THE CZECH AMERICANS

THE GERMAN AMERICANS

THE GREEK AMERICANS

THE HAITIAN AMERICANS

ILLEGAL ALIENS

THE IRISH AMERICANS

THE ITALIAN AMERICANS

THE JAPANESE AMERICANS

THE JEWISH AMERICANS

THE KOREAN AMERICANS

THE LEBANESE CHRISTIANS

THE MEXICAN AMERICANS

THE POLISH AMERICANS

THE PUERTO RICANS

THE RUSSIAN AMERICANS

Other titles in preparation

## CHELSEA HOUSE PUBLISHERS

# A
# NATION OF
# NATIONS

### Daniel Patrick Moynihan

The Constitution of the United States begins: "We the People of the United States. . . ." Yet, as we know, the United States was not then and is not now made up of a single group of people. It is made up of many peoples. Immigrants and bondsmen from Europe, Asia, Africa, and Central and South America came here or were brought here, and still they come. They forged one nation and made it their own. More than 100 years ago, Walt Whitman expressed this great central fact of America: "Here is not merely a nation, but a teeming Nation of nations."

Although the ingenuity and acts of courage of these immigrants, our ancestors, shaped the North American way of life, we sometimes take their contributions for granted. This fine series, *The Immigrant Experience,* examines the experiences and contributions of different immigrant groups and how these contributions determined the future of the United States and Canada.

Immigrants did not abandon their ethnic traditions when they reached the shores of North America. Each ethnic group had its own customs and traditions, and each brought different experiences, accomplishments, skills, values, styles of dress, and tastes in food that lingered long after its arrival. Yet this profusion of differences created a singularity, or bond, among the immigrants.

The United States and Canada are unusual in this respect. Whereas religious and ethnic differences have sparked intolerance throughout the rest of the world—from the 17th-century religious wars to the 19th-century nationalist movements in Europe to the near extermination of the Jewish people under Nazi Germany—North Americans have struggled to learn how to respect each other's differences and live in harmony.

Our two countries are hardly the only two in which different groups must learn to live together. There is no nation of significant size anywhere in the world which would not be classified as multiethnic. But only in North America are there so *many* different groups, most of them living cheek by jowl with one another.

This is not easy. Look around the world. And it has not always been easy for us. Witness the exclusion of Chinese immigrants, and for practical purposes Japanese also, in the late 19th century. But by the late 20th century, Chinese and Japanese Americans were the most successful of all the groups recorded by the census. We have had prejudice aplenty, but it has been resisted and recurrently overcome.

The remarkable ability of Americans to live together as one people was seriously threatened by the issue of slavery. Thousands of settlers from the British Isles had arrived in the colonies as indentured servants, agreeing to work for a specified number of years on farms or as apprentices in return for passage to America and room and board. When the first Africans arrived in the then-British colonies during the 17th century, some colonists thought that they too should be treated as indentured servants. Eventually, the question of whether the Africans should be treated as indentured, like the English, or as slaves who could be owned for life was considered in a Maryland court. The court's calamitous decree held that blacks were slaves bound to a lifelong servitude, and so also were their children. America went through a time of moral examination and civil war before it finally freed African slaves and their descendants. The principle that all people are created equal had faced its greatest challenge and survived.

Yet the court ruling that set blacks apart from other races fanned flames of discrimination that burned long after slavery was abolished—and that still flicker today. Indeed, it was about the time of the American Civil War that European theories of evolution were turned to the service of ranking different peoples by their presumed distance from our apelike ancestors.

When the Irish flooded American cities to escape the famine in Ireland, the cartoonists caricatured the typical "Paddy" (a common term for Irish immigrants) as an apelike creature with jutting jaw and sloping forehead.

By the 20th century, racism and ethnic prejudice had given rise to virulent theories of a Northern European master race. When Adolf Hitler came to power in Germany in 1933, he popularized the notion of an Aryan race. Only a man of the deepest ignorance and evil could have done this. *Aryan* is a Sanskrit word, which is to say the ancient script of what we now think of as India. It means "noble" and was adopted by linguists—notably by a fine German scholar, Max Müller—to denote the Indo-European family of languages. Müller was horrified that anyone could think of it in terms of race, especially a race of blond-haired, blue-eyed Teutons. But the Nazis embraced the notion of a master race. Anyone with darker and heavier features was considered inferior. Buttressed by these theories, the German Nazi state from 1933 to 1945 set out to destroy European Jews, along with Poles, Gypsies, Russians, and other groups considered inferior. It nearly succeeded. Millions of these people were murdered.

The tragedies brought on by ethnic and racial intolerance throughout the world demonstrate the importance of North America's efforts to create a society free of prejudice and inequality.

A relatively recent example of the New World's desire to resolve ethnic friction nonviolently is the solution that the Canadians found to a conflict between two ethnic groups. A long-standing dispute as to whether Canadian culture was properly

English or French resurfaced in the mid-1960s, dividing the peoples of the French-speaking Province of Quebec from those of the English-speaking provinces. Relations grew tense, then bitter, then violent. The Royal Commission on Bilingualism and Biculturalism was established to study the growing crisis and to propose measures to ease the tensions. As a result of the commission's recommendations, all official documents and statements from the national government's capital at Ottawa are now issued in both French and English, and bilingual education is encouraged.

The year 1980 marked a coming of age for the United States's ethnic heritage. For the first time, the U.S. Bureau of the Census asked people about their ethnic background. Americans chose from more than 100 groups, including French Basque, Spanish Basque, French Canadian, African American, Peruvian, Armenian, Chinese, and Japanese. The ethnic group with the largest response was English (49.6 million). More than 100 million Americans claimed ancestors from the British Isles, which includes England, Ireland, Wales, and Scotland. There were almost as many Germans (49.2 million) as English. The Irish-American population (40.2 million) was third, but the next-largest ethnic group, the African Americans, was a distant fourth (21 million). There was a sizable group of French ancestry (13 million) as well as of Italian (12 million). Poles, Dutch, Swedes, Norwegians, and Russians followed. These groups, and other smaller ones, represent the wondrous profusion of ethnic influences in North America.

Canada too has learned more about the diversity of its population. Studies conducted during the French/English conflict showed that Canadians were descended from Ukrainians, Germans, Italians, Chinese, Japanese, native Indians, and Inuit, among others. Canada found it had no ethnic majority, although nearly half of its immigrant population had come from the British Isles. Canada, like the United States, is a land of immigrants for whom mutual tolerance is a matter of reason as well as principle. But note how difficult this can be in practice, even for persons of manifest goodwill.

The people of North America are the descendants of one of the greatest migrations in history. And that migration is not over. Koreans, Vietnamese, Nicaraguans, Cubans, and many others are heading for the shores of North America in large numbers. This mix of cultures shapes every aspect of our lives. To understand ourselves, we must know something about our diverse ethnic ancestry. Nothing so defines the North American nations as the motto on the Great Seal of the United States: *E Pluribus Unum*—Out of Many, One.

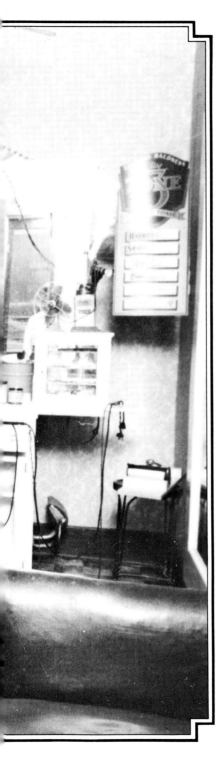

*Steve Safranck stands in the barbershop he ran for 40 years in Wilber, Nebraska, home to many Czech Americans.*

# A NEW BEGINNING

I n the 1880s and 1890s nearly 100,000 Czechs emigrated to America. They left behind no unified nation to call their own. Czechs came from the central European regions of Bohemia and Moravia, which comprise most of the present-day Czech Republic. At the time when Czechs began to reach American shores, Bohemia and Moravia were controlled by the Hapsburg Empire, which had governed the Czech homeland for centuries.

Unlike many other Slavic immigrants, Czechs arrived on American shores both skilled and literate, able to function with ease in both the city and the country. In urban enclaves such as New York and Chicago, Czech immigrants found work in the cigar-making or garment-manufacturing industries. Because Czechs preferred to settle on the city outskirts, they can claim to be some of America's first suburbanites. They established neighborhoods with one- and two-family houses, grocery stores, and other local businesses. The Czech districts in most cities were almost totally self-sufficient: Residents bought their necessities in Czech-owned shops, transacted business through Czech savings and loan companies, attended schools that taught both Czech and English, and often conducted daily business in Czech.

*A sign in both Czech and English welcomes travelers to Wilber.*

Those Czechs who headed for rural America cleared wooded land and planted grain. They developed thousands of acres of land for cultivation, thus opening up the Midwest to further settlement. Czech pioneers founded dozens of towns such as Milligan, Nebraska; Pilsen, Iowa; and New Prague and Litomysy, both located in Minnesota. Czechs also established a large community in Texas.

As the 19th century gave way to the 20th, Czechs gradually entered the mainstream of American life, but they also sought to preserve their traditional customs and culture. Many joined gymnastic societies known as *sokols*, which encouraged young people to develop discipline and national pride as well as physical fitness. Tens of thousands of Czech Americans belonged to fraternal societies, which provided financial support in times of need and also brought Czech immigrants together with their compatriots.

By the waning years of the 20th century, more than 120,000 Czechs belonged to fraternal organizations. Czechs today also preserve their heritage by holding festivals throughout the United States. There Czechs—and Americans of all backgrounds—enjoy Czech food, music, and dance. And, of course, everyone joins in for a hearty polka, a dance invented by a Czech band.

Czech Americans number almost 1.3 million, spread throughout the entire United States—including Hawaii. Nearly half are concentrated in the north-central states such as Illinois (including the largest number in any one city, Chicago), Wisconsin, Ohio, Minnesota, and Nebraska. Many also live in California, but the largest number of Czechs, roughly 190,000, can be found in Texas, where they publish several Czech newspapers and periodicals.

Today, Czech culture in America is enjoying a revival, spurred in part by the influx of Czech refugees who have arrived since World War II. Each year hundreds of Czechs ask for permanent residency status. Czech intellectuals and artists—who are among the most prominent members of the new Czech immigration—are as determined as were earlier genera-

tions of Czech Americans to preserve their culture in their new homeland. Their success attests not only to the strength of the Czechs as a people but also to the freedom they have found in the United States. In maintaining their own heritage, Czech Americans have strengthened and enriched American society. Through the efforts of generations of Czech immigrants, Czech culture has become a part of America.

*Rose Meisel (seated, far left), a Czech refugee from World War II, poses with co-workers at a Royal Canadian Air Force base in the Canadian town of Trenton. Meisel oversaw rationing on the base from 1943 to 1945.*

# A PROUD HISTORY

The Czechs are a Slavic people who inhabit the Czech Republic. Located in central Europe, the Czech Republic is bordered by Poland and Germany to the north and west, Austria to the south, and Slovakia to the east. Its location has been a blessing and a curse. On one hand, the Czechs have benefited from exposure to Western European cultural and intellectual currents, such as the Renaissance and the Enlightenment. On the other hand, the Czechs have often been conquered by foreign invaders. Although Czechs have often lived under the domination of foreigners, they have always succeeded in preserving their own identity and culture.

For most of the 20th century (1918–93), the Czech homeland was part of the nation of Czechoslovakia. In 1918, Czechoslovakia was formed when members of two Slavic ethnic groups—the Czechs and the Slovaks—united four independent regions: Bohemia, Moravia, Slovakia, and part of Silesia. Within the new state, each group tended to remain in those areas it had traditionally inhabited. Most Slovaks stayed in Slovakia, and the majority of Czechs continued to live in Bohemia and Moravia.

The history of the Czech people predates the formation of Czechoslovakia by more than 1,000 years. During the height of the Roman Empire (A.D. 14–280),

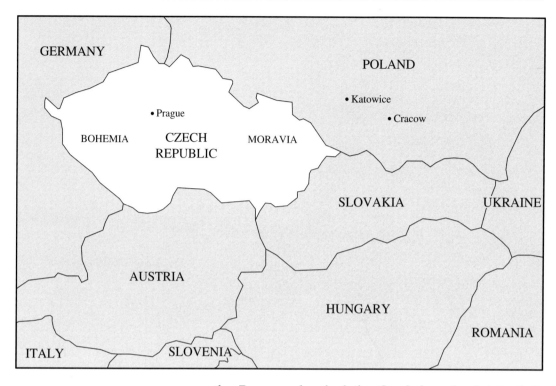

the Romans absorbed the Czech homeland into their vast domain, which stretched across the European continent. They called the western part of Czechoslovakia "Boihemum," after the Boii, a Celtic tribe that inhabited the region. Known to English speakers as Bohemia, this region today composes roughly two-thirds of the land mass of the Czech Republic.

Bohemia became home to Slavic people in the 5th century, when ancestors of the modern Czechs first settled in the region. By the 9th century, the Slavs had established Great Moravia, which served as home to the Czechs, the Slovaks, and their neighbors, the Moravians. Great Moravia grew from a state into an empire that included the present-day Czech Republic, Slovakia, southern Poland, and northern Hungary. Although Czechs paid homage to Moravian monarchs, they enjoyed great independence within the empire and were governed by Czech monarchs such as Queen Libuše. According to Czech legend, Queen Libuše took a peasant named Přemysl as her husband. Together they united their homeland into a single duchy and established Bohemia's earliest dynasty, the Přemyslid rulers. During this time the Czechs were also converted to Christianity, largely as the result of the work of two Greek missionaries, Cyril and Methodius, the Apostles to the Slavs, who were dispatched to Moravia in 863. Cyril and Methodius allowed their Slavic converts to say the Mass in Slavonic rather than Latin, as the Roman Catholic church usually mandated for its followers. Differences on the language of worship and other matters would soon lead to a schism between the Roman and Eastern branches of Catholicism.

## The Kingdom of Bohemia

The Great Moravian Empire flourished for about 100 years, but in the 10th century it fell to two foreign powers: the Holy Roman Empire, located in what is now Germany, and the kingdom of Hungary. Germans and Hungarians divided the Great Moravian Em-

*An 11th-century fresco shows the missionaries Cyril and Methodius kneeling before Christ, two angels, and Saints Andrew and Clement. The fresco decorates the crypt of Cyril, who died in Rome in A.D. 869.*

*Holy Roman Emperor Charles IV, also known as Charles of Luxembourg, established the hereditary monarchy in Bohemia and presided over a golden age of Czech culture.*

pire between themselves. Hungary swallowed up Slovakia, and the Holy Roman Emperor Otto I claimed Bohemia and Moravia. Under the influence of the Holy Roman Empire, Czechs came under the sway of the Roman Catholic church.

In general, the Holy Roman emperors allowed the Czechs considerable freedom. In 1198, during the reign of Přemyslid king Otakar I, Bohemia became an independent kingdom that included Moravia and most of Silesia among its territories. During the next century the young kingdom expanded rapidly until it stretched from the Adriatic Sea to the Oder River. This growth raised the young kingdom to a new position of eminence within Europe. In 1355, Bohemia's prestige increased yet again when one of its monarchs, Charles I—who had first ascended to the throne in 1346—was crowned Holy Roman emperor. As Emperor Charles IV, he ruled both the kingdom of Bohemia and the Holy Roman Empire from the Czech capital of Prague.

During Charles's reign Bohemia enjoyed an age of economic prosperity and cultural vitality unknown at any other time in its history. Art and architecture thrived, as did education. In 1348, Charles founded the first university in central Europe, Charles University. It remains one of Europe's greatest institutions of higher learning.

Charles also penned one of the most important documents in Czech history, the Golden Bull. The Golden Bull clearly established a line of succession to the Bohemian monarchy and also defined the role of Bohemia's king within the Holy Roman Empire. According to historian S. Harrison Thompson, the Golden Bull "secured the internal independence of Bohemia from interference by the [Holy Roman Empire] . . . "

## The Hussite Movement

Charles IV—known to Czech history as the father of his country—laid the foundations of an autonomous government within Bohemia. After Charles's death in 1378 the cause of an independent Bohemia gained momentum under the leadership of Jan Hus. Born in

1369, Hus served as a rector at Charles University and soon developed a reputation as one of Prague's greatest orators. His sermons, which drew large crowds, condemned the wealth and worldliness of the Roman Catholic church. Hus criticized Bohemia's bishops for neglecting the basic duties of the priesthood, and he pledged to reform the church in order to restore such true Christian virtues as simplicity and piety.

Hus soon attracted a large following, but when he refused to temper his criticisms, he was excommunicated. He continued preaching and eventually broadened his cause to include not only the reform of the church in Bohemia but also the liberation of Bohemia from the Holy Roman Empire. Hus's message gained enormous popularity within Bohemia, in part because many Czechs equated freedom from the Holy Roman Empire with liberation from the powerful German aristocrats who controlled much of Bohemia's wealth and power. In 1415 the Holy Roman Emperor Sigismund offered Hus the opportunity to present his views before a council of nobles and powerful churchmen. He granted Hus a writ of safe conduct, but when Hus appeared he was arrested and then condemned to burn at the stake for heresy.

But Hus had inspired a national fervor among the Czech masses. The efforts of his followers, known as the Hussites, to carry on his crusade for reform led to war. During the Hussite Wars, which lasted for more

*Charles University in Prague, founded by Charles IV in 1348, remains an important center of learning.*

*Czech religious reformer Jan Hus, whose work is considered a precursor to the Protestant Reformation, was burned at the stake for heresy in 1414.*

than 100 years, the Hussites clashed with three powerful forces: the Roman Catholic church, the wealthy Germans living within Bohemia, and the kingdom's feudal lords, all of whom opposed religious and social change in Bohemia. Because the majority of the Germans within Bohemia were Catholics, the Hussites' anti-Catholicism was fueled in part by their resentment of the Germans who had pushed into the heart of the Czech homeland and settled there. According to Edvard Beneš, who served as president of Czechoslovakia in the 1930s, "At bottom the struggle was Catholic against Protestant, but since the Germans were Catholics and the Czechs persisted in remaining heretics [dissenters from established church dogma], the contest naturally assumed a racial character."

Led by the military genius Jan Žižka, who was then 60 years old and nearly blind, the Hussites battled legions of armies dispatched to Bohemia by Sigismund. Hus's followers adopted the motto *Pravda Vítězí* (The truth will win), a credo revived centuries later by the Czechoslovak republic. Drawing on a inchoate spirit of nationalism, the Hussites eventually won the loyalty of the vast majority of the Czech populace, many of whom volunteered to fight against the Holy Roman Empire's powerful army. In contrast to the trained troops of Sigismund and his successors, most Hussite brigades were composed of peasants and towns-people. Despite early victories over the powerful armies of Germany, Austria, and Hungary, the Bohemians were ultimately forced to accept Sigismund as their king in 1436. Although the wars dragged on for more than another century, the Holy Roman Empire and its allies had broken the back of the Hussite movement.

## "We Were All Hussites"

The Hussite Wars helped set the stage for another radical movement that swept through Europe during the 1500s—the Protestant Reformation. Like the Hussite movement, the Protestant Reformation—sparked in 1514 by a German priest named Martin Luther—criticized Roman Catholic doctrine and the authority of the church hierarchy. Luther himself said, "We were all Hussites without being aware of it," thus acknowledging his debt to the teachings of Jan Hus and the many similarities between the two movements.

*An engraving from* Ceski-Moravska Kronica, *a Czech history book, shows Czech patriot Jan Žižka (left).*

The Protestant Reformation attracted thousands of Czechs, including many among Bohemia's nobility. Once again, religious conflict flared up in Bohemia when a Catholic monarch, Archduke Ferdinand I of Austria, ascended to the kingdom's throne in 1526. A member of the powerful Hapsburg dynasty, whose empire spanned much of western and central Europe, Ferdinand tried to force Roman Catholicism on Bohemia's Protestant nobles. In 1618 tensions between the Hapsburgs and the Czech aristocrats erupted into the Thirty Years' War.

The conflict spread throughout most of central and eastern Europe, but it was particularly devastating to

*Martin Luther, whose demands for reform of the Catholic church began the Reformation. Luther acknowledged the Hussites as the spiritual forerunners of the Protestants.*

the Czech Protestant nobility. In one of the most tragic incidents in Czech history, a contingent of Bohemian Protestants was crushed by the forces of Hapsburg emperor Ferdinand II on a hill known as the White Mountain, located outside Prague, in 1620. The battle represented a decisive step in the subordination of the people of central and eastern Europe. The defeat of the Czech Protestants effectively obliterated the Czech national movement begun by Hus two centuries before. The Hapsburgs declared Roman Catholicism the sole faith of Bohemia and elevated their native tongue, German, to the status of an official state language that was used in commerce, courts, and classrooms.

*In 1663, French artist Jacques Callot detailed the horrors of the Thirty Years' War in this engraving, entitled* Grandes Misères de la Guerre *(The Great Miseries of War).*

## The Loss of Identity

The Thirty Years' War eliminated nearly all Bohemia's Czech nobility. Hapsburg forces evicted aristocratic families from their homes, searched their possessions for books advocating Protestantism, and burned the "heretical" texts in the public square to "eradicate the devil" of Reformation. Worse, the Hapsburgs sent more than 30,000 leading families into exile abroad. Most exiled Czechs chose to settle in neighboring countries such as Russia, but many also sought refuge in the Netherlands. The estates of the deposed Czech nobility were given to German Catholic aristocrats who had supported the Hapsburg cause.

The Thirty Years' War devastated not only the aristocracy but also the Czech population at large. Nearly one-third of the Czech population had been killed by war's end, in 1648. The survivors suffered many indignities under the Hapsburgs, including oppressive taxes that forced the peasants into poverty. The Hapsburgs used the tax revenue to fund their huge military, which by the mid-1600s was enforcing Hapsburg rule across most of east-central Europe. Thousands of young Czechs were forced to leave home in the prime of their life to serve in the hated Hapsburg armies.

The Hapsburg state demanded much of the Czechs but gave them little in return. Hapsburg monarchs Ferdinand III, Leopold I, Joseph I, and Charles VI—who successively ruled the empire from 1637 to 1740—denied Czechs higher education and almost completely reversed the cultural advances Czechs had made under Charles IV. Czech hardship eased little during the reign of Maria Theresa, who from 1740 to 1780 controlled both Bohemia and Hungary from the empire's capital city of Vienna. In order to standardize government documents, Maria Theresa established German as the sole official language of Bohemia.

## A New Nationalism

In attempting to Germanize the Czechs, Maria Theresa unwittingly helped revive their determination to preserve their language and culture. During the mid-1800s great advances were made in the study of the Czech language, and its use as both a written and spoken tongue was promoted. Josef Dobrovský, an expert in the field of linguistics, codified Czech; Josef Jungmann compiled the first Czech dictionary; and František Palacký wrote a chronicle of the Czech people in their

*Hapsburg empress Maria Theresa and her husband, Francis I, sit surrounded by their 11 children in a portrait by Martin Meytens.*

own language. Palacký attempted to dignify Czech history by calling the Hussite Wars precursors of the American and French revolutions. The work of these three men built on earlier efforts by Jan Hus, who greatly simplified the Czech language through the use of diacritical marks.

The Czechs were not isolated in their efforts to revive an ancestral culture. Throughout the 19th century many central European ethnic groups worked toward a similar goal, inspired by a continental movement known as nationalism—the belief that nations and ethnic groups should retain their traditional language, customs, and culture. Indeed, the achievements of men such as Jungmann and Palacký helped bring about a cultural reawakening of the Czech people. By the 1840s, music and literature with Czech themes had gained an enthusiastic following among a group long

*Czech author František Palacký produced the first history of Bohemia written in the Czech language.*

deprived of its traditional identity. This progress continued for several decades. The 1880s saw the widespread use of Czech in many Bohemian schools and regions. At Charles University, nationalists won a victory when students gained the right to a separate Czech-speaking faculty.

The 19th century in Europe was known for its revolutionary fervor as well as its nationalistic spirit. In 1848 protests against political oppression swept through the Hapsburg Empire, reaching Bohemia in

March of that year. Thousands assembled in Prague to demand constitutional rights for Bohemia. Czechs drew up petitions demanding autonomy for Bohemia within the Hapsburg Empire. They also called for equality of Czech and German languages, the regulation of wages, and the abolition of feudalism, a medieval landholding system that concentrated land ownership in the hands of the aristocracy and bound the peasants to the nobles' estates as agricultural laborers.

The Czechs succeeded in winning some concessions from the Hapsburgs. But when control of the Hapsburg Empire was divided among Austria and Hungary in 1876 by virtue of the creation of the Dual Monarchy, the Czech quest for independence was slowed. The Hapsburg lands were divided between

*Czech patriots erect a barricade during the March 1848 uprising against Hapsburg rule. The failure of the uprising inspired many Czechs, particularly among the lower middle class, to immigrate to the United States in search of political freedom.*

governments located in Vienna and Budapest, the capital of Hungary. The Czechs remained under the control of Vienna, but the Slovaks were governed by Budapest. The resulting fragmentation, coupled with a consolidation of its power by the Austrian government, hindered the Czechs' attempts to develop a national consciousness. The Czechs would not free themselves from Hapsburg rule until the beginning of the 20th century.

## The Formation of Czechoslovakia

During World War I, which began in 1914, Czech patriots worked toward liberation by assisting in the defeat of the Austro-Hungarian Empire. They were indirectly aided in their struggle by Czech immigrants living in the United States and Canada. These New World Czechs joined forces with Slovak immigrants seeking independence for their homeland from Hungary. Czech and Slovak leaders signed the Cleveland Agreement (1915) and the Pittsburgh Agreement

*A propaganda poster from World War I shows a Czech in uniform attacking a German soldier with a bayonet. It reads, "At the Assassins! Hurray for Democracy!"*

HRR NA VRAHA!

ZA DEMOKRACII!

*Tomáš Masaryk was a professor of philosophy before becoming the first president of Czechoslovakia in 1918.*

(1918) in which they pledged to fight Austria-Hungary by supporting the Allies (chiefly France, Britain, Russia, and the United States) with soldiers and money.

The two agreements also introduced the idea of an independent Czechoslovak state. The patriots hoped that if the Allies defeated the Central Powers (Germany and Austria-Hungary), the Czechs and Slovaks would be permitted to create a new federated state, Czechoslovakia. According to the Cleveland and Pittsburgh agreements, the Czechs and Slovaks were to have equal roles in governing the new nation.

The Czech contingent found a leader in Tomáš Garrigue Masaryk. A member of the Czech parliament, Masaryk left his homeland at the beginning of World War I in order to organize for the creation of an independent Czech state. He traveled to the United

States to visit with President Woodrow Wilson and helped unite the North American Czechs and Slovaks behind the cause of an independent Czechoslovakia. Masaryk soon saw this goal realized. On October 28, 1918, in Geneva, Switzerland, a provisional government headed by Masaryk proclaimed Czechoslovakia an independent state. When Prague followed suit, the Republic of Czechoslovakia was born.

## Hard Times for the New Republic

Czechs rejoiced in achieving their independence at last, but the Slovaks did not necessarily share their happiness. Because the Czechs outnumbered them by more than two to one in the new state, the Slovaks had argued for the creation of their own, autonomous government. Masaryk at first agreed to this arrangement and even wrote it into the Pittsburgh and Cleveland pacts, but in the end he advocated a unified nation. In 1920 the new Czechoslovak parliament created a united Czechoslovakia.

The Czech majority in the parliament soon learned that they could not silence the Slovaks by outvoting them. Dissent from the Slovak citizenry—represented by the Slovak People's party—created a rift within the young democracy that seriously weakened it. Conflict arose not only between the Czechs and the Slovaks but also between the Czechs and other ethnic minorities living within Czechoslovakia: the Germans and the Magyars (Hungarians). The new republic became a battleground of warring factions, each of which viewed the others with distrust and even hatred.

By the 1930s the new nation's domestic ills left it vulnerable to attack from a traditional enemy, Germany. Germans had resided on Czech lands since the medieval Bohemian-Moravian state had invited them to settle in the border region known as the Sudetenland. After the formation of Czechoslovakia, Sudeten Germans, resentful of Czech rule, advocated incorporation into Germany proper. Germany's Nazi dictator, Adolf Hitler, saw the unrest of the Sudeten Germans as an opportunity for conquest and in February 1938 declared himself "the protector of those Germans who

*The Czech parliament in session on October 7, 1919. Regional differences threatened to divide the new nation almost from its first days of independence.*

are subject to another country." After threatening Czechoslovakia with invasion, Hitler concluded the Munich Pact with Great Britain, Italy, and France in October 1938. By its terms Czechoslovakia was forced to cede its western provinces, including the Sudetenland, to Germany. Poland soon made similar land claims on behalf of Poles living within Czechoslovakia, as did Hungary. Altogether Czechoslovakia lost territories inhabited by almost 5 million people, 24 percent of whom were Czechs or Slovaks.

The French and British governments hoped that the Sudetenland would appease Hitler, but they were mistaken. Hitler hungered for more than the Sudetenland alone and hoped to control all the Czech and Slovak territory that Germany had ruled during the days of the Holy Roman Empire. In March 1939 he achieved his aim by forcing Czech president Emil Hácha to sur-

*Angry crowds of Czechs greeted Nazi troops when they rolled into Prague on March 15, 1939.*

render the provinces of Bohemia and Moravia to Germany. Hitler then granted Slovakia independence, but in reality it was nothing more than a Nazi satellite state.

## Communism

After the outbreak of World War II, Czechoslovakia's former president Edvard Beneš—whose presidency fell between that of Masaryk and Hácha—advanced the cause of Czech nationalism from exile in England. Beneš set up a provisional government in London, where he helped organize Czech units to fight with the Allied forces against Nazi Germany. Czech soldiers and civilians bravely fought the Nazi troops, but the Germans easily quashed the Czech resistance. The Nazi retaliation was brutal and horrifying, especially in the village of Lidice, where they exterminated virtually the entire population.

Beneš tried to organize a new Czech liberation movement from his office in London, but he found little support among Western nations. In 1943 he journeyed to Moscow and met with Joseph Stalin, the premier of the Soviet Union. Beneš asked Stalin to help reunite the Czechs and Slovaks into a new Czechoslovakia after Hitler's defeat. In return Beneš promised that he would allow Czech Communists to participate in the postwar Czechoslovak government.

In fact, after World War II Czech Communists emerged as the strongest national party in their homeland, which had been restored to its pre-1938 borders

*On May 12, 1943, Czech president Edvard Beneš met with U.S. president Franklin Roosevelt in the Oval Office in the White House to discuss the postwar future of Czechoslovakia.*

by virtue of agreements reached during the Potsdam Conference of 1945. In the election of 1946 Czech Communists obtained more than one-third of the nation's vote and established a coalition government led by Klement Gottwald. Edvard Beneš was elected Czechoslovakia's president.

The Communists, unwilling to share power, staged huge demonstrations and gained control of the nation's trade unions and police force. The supposed suicide of Jan Masaryk, son of the former president, demoralized the opposition. After provoking a political crisis, the Communists forced Beneš's resignation and took power. Thousands of Czechs were arrested for alleged political crimes and sent to forced labor camps.

The repression eased somewhat with the death of Stalin in 1953. Politicians, writers, and academics targeted for repression began to call for political and economic reform. When the leader of the Czech reform

*Czech president Václav Havel addresses legislators from both houses of the Czech Parliament after they elected him to a second term in office January 20, 1998. Havel was elected to his first term as president of the Czech Republic in January 1993 after the breakup of the nation of Czechoslovakia.*

movement, Alexander Dubček, became head of the Czechoslovak Communist party in January 1968, he instituted "socialism with a human face," lifting censorship restrictions during this brief "Prague Spring." However, in August 1968, 650,000 Soviet and Eastern bloc forces invaded Czechoslovakia, ousted Dubček, and replaced him with Gustáv Husák, a Slovak whom many regarded as a puppet of the Soviet regime.

Dissent was not stifled for long. In 1977, the opposition drafted Charter 77, demanding that the Czechoslovak government live up to human rights documents it had signed. After Mikhail Gorbachev became Soviet premier in 1985 and loosened control over Eastern Europe, the pressure for reform increased. In 1989, the signers of Charter 77 and others formed the Civic Forum under the leadership of dissident playwright Václav Havel. Husák (then president) and party head Milos Jakes resigned in December, and Havel took over as president, completing what came to be known as the "Velvet Revolution."

Following free elections in 1990, which swept Civic Forum and its Slovak equivalent, Public Against Violence, to power, the Slovakians began to clamor for autonomy. On January 1, 1993, despite Havel's resistance, the nation split into two new republics—the Czech Republic and Slovakia. Havel was elected Czech president, a popular but largely ceremonial position, with Václav Klaus as prime minister and head of government. The Velvet Revolution and its aftermath had established two democratic states to replace a single authoritarian one.

The Moravian settlement of Bethlehem, Pennsylvania, is depicted in an 18th-century engraving by British artist Paul Sandby.

# THE EARLIEST ARRIVALS

The story of Czech migration to North America in many ways mirrors the history of the Czechs in their homeland. Most Czechs immigrated to North America during times of religious or political repression or economic deprivation. This pattern of migration began in the 1630s, when the first Czech immigrants—Protestant aristocrats—arrived in the New World. These early Czech Americans numbered very few. Most settled in colonies established by other European nations, such as New Sweden (today Wilmington, Delaware) and New Amsterdam (now New York). In fact, Czech was one of the 18 chronicled spoken languages in New York in the mid-1600s.

The early colonial Czech community included several prominent members, the most famous of whom, Augustine Herman, has become a figure of near-legendary stature within America's Czech community. In 1618, two years before the Battle of White Mountain, the 13-year-old Herman and his family left Bohemia and crossed Europe to Amsterdam, where Herman apprenticed as a surveyor and began working for the Dutch West India Company. In 1633 his employers offered him the chance to travel to North America. Soon after his arrival in New Amsterdam, Herman established a successful business as a fur trader, one of

*Fur trader, tobacco merchant, mapmaker, and surveyor Augustine Herman was the first Czech immigrant to rise to prominence in colonial America.*

the most common professions in the Dutch colony. With his partner, George Hack, Herman also became the largest exporter of tobacco in North America.

In 1659, border disputes in Maryland between the Dutch and the English led Governor Peter Stuyvesant to call for Herman and his skills as a surveyor. Herman was so taken with the beauty of the Atlantic coastline that he offered to make a complete map of the area in exchange for land there. He spent 10 years surveying and charting the mid-Atlantic coastline, producing a map of "Virginia and Maryland as it is Planted and Inhabited in this present Year 1670 Surveyed and Exactly Drawne by the Only Labour and Endeavour of

Augustin Herman, Bohemiensis." Herman earned 13,000 acres of land for his cartographic skills, and on this estate he built a house called Bohemia Manor, on what is now the Bohemia River.

Augustine Herman's keen business sense, coupled with his skills as surveyor and mapmaker, enabled him to achieve success in America. Later, other Czechs who had a similar motivation to settle and succeed would also do well in the New World. But the first substantial migration of Czechs to North America was composed of men and women seeking not economic opportunity but religious freedom.

## The Moravians

Although individual Czech names are hard to locate in the annals of immigration, Czechs were almost certainly represented in the group of Moravian Brethren who arrived in America from England between 1741 and 1762. Historians estimate that more than 700 Moravians established settlements in Pennsylvania, North Carolina, and Georgia. The Moravian Brethren traced their heritage back to the Czech and German Hussites

*Augustine Herman's map of the Virginia and Maryland coastlines earned him 13,000 acres of land and the admiration of his contemporaries.*

who fought in the Thirty Years' War. When after the war the victorious Hapsburgs drove the Moravians and many other Protestant sects out of Bohemia and Moravia, the Brethren scattered all over Europe. In England their belief in pacifism earned them a cool welcome. By the mid-1700s Moravians in England realized that they could not remain there, and they began to consider immigration to England's colonies in North America. In 1740, George Whitefield, a British Protestant who helped found the Methodist Church, offered a group of Moravian Brethren free passage to Philadelphia on his sloop. The Moravians Whitefield brought to America founded the Pennsylvania towns of Bethlehem, Nazareth, and Lititz (originally Lidice). Later on they established colonies in North Carolina and Georgia.

By the time of the American War of Independence nearly 2,500 Moravian Brethren lived within the 13 colonies, where they had established a reputation as ef-

*An illustration from a history book shows members of the Moravian Brethren teaching black slaves the rites of Christianity. The Brethren also did much missionary work among the Native Americans.*

*George Whitefield led a religious revival, known as the Great Awakening, in the colonies. It was Whitefield who was instrumental in bringing the Moravian Brethren to America.*

fective educators. In addition to setting up elementary and secondary schools, the Brethren founded Moravian College in Bethlehem, one of the oldest institutions of higher learning in America today. They also organized the first interdenominational college for women in America.

The Moravian Brethren's educational philosophy—unusually progressive for its time—owes much to the influence of Jan Ámos Komenský, a Czech proponent of educational reform. Born in 1592, Komenský, better known by his Latin name of Comenius, served as the last bishop of the Moravian Brethren before fleeing Bohemia after the Battle of White Mountain. Komenský made his home in Holland, where he soon gained fame by advocating vocational education instead of traditional academic schooling. Komenský's philosophy appealed to the Moravian Brethren, who used voca-

IOHAN-AMOS COMENIVS MORAVVS·A·ÆTAT·60. 1652

*Loe, here an Exile, who to serue his God,*
*Hath sharply tasted of proud Pashurs Rod,*
*Whose learning, Piety, & true worth beeing knowne*
*To all the world, makes all the world his owne.*

*The teachings of Jan Komenský, known as Comenius, instilled a high regard for formal education in the Moravian Brethren.*

tional training in their schools. His belief that "no reason can be shown why the female sex . . . should be kept from a knowledge of language and wisdom" also found favor with the Brethren.

The Moravians also displayed a keen interest in medicine, and a typical Moravian community in the New World almost always featured a hospital. These medical centers played an important role in the American colonists' struggle against England because wounded patriots regularly received care in them and obtained supplies to carry to the battlefront.

The Brethren eased the lives of colonists, too, by acting as intermediaries between whites and Native Americans. Moravians were among the few Europeans to win the trust of American Indians, many of whom attended Moravian-founded mission schools. Indian missions were so successful that one is still in existence today. The religious education provided in frontier settlements and in the Indian missions included a solid foundation in sacred music, especially hymn singing. The relatively tiny Moravian settlements in Pennsylvania and North Carolina produced a surprisingly large body of religious music. In 1744, for example, the Bethlehem, Pennsylvania, community organized the first symphonic orchestra in America. A decade later the Moravian Trombone Choir—which claims the longest continuous existence of any musical group in the United States—began performing.

Protestant churches still reflect the influence of the Moravian Brethren. Today almost 50,000 Americans claim membership in the Moravian church. Together with other Protestant sects, they keep alive the great repertory of church and classical music brought to this country by the Moravian Brethren. The hard work and dedication of the Moravian Brethren enabled them to enrich not only their own lives but also the lives of fellow Americans.

*Czech farmers in Wilber,
Nebraska, pose on the land of
John Richtarik in 1909. Czech
immigrants were attracted to the
Midwest by the prospect of
owning their own land.*

# A WAVE OF IMMIGRATION

Approximately 100 years after the Moravian Brethren set foot on American soil, Czechs belonging to another segment of society—the military—engineered a dramatic escape to the United States. In 1847 about 40 Czech soldiers fled an army fortress in Mainz (in what is now Germany) and set out for North America. These Czech soldiers deserted an army that virtually enslaved the young men of Bohemia by forcing them to serve in the military.

The mutinous soldiers composed just one part of a small movement of political refugees who left Bohemia for the United States during the first half of the 1800s. Others included Bohemian intellectuals who had participated in the nationalist revival of the 1840s and 1850s. Doctors, professors, composers, and journalists left their homeland by the score to escape the repression of Hapsburg rule. By 1850 about 500 members of the Czech intelligentsia had journeyed to U.S. shores. Among these newcomers was Jan Nepomuk Neumann. Born in Bohemia in 1811, Neumann helped found the American parochial school system and was honored by the Roman Catholic church in 1977, when he was canonized as the first American saint.

But the vast majority of the Czechs who immigrated to the United States between 1850 and 1890 came to escape hunger, not political oppression. Although Europe's population boomed during the early

*Peasants carrying beet leaves— used as cattle feed—pause on the outskirts of Brunn, a town in Moravia, in about 1900.*

decades of the 19th century, the amount of arable land remained the same or even diminished, and the existing technology did not enable food production to keep pace with the growth in population. In the 1840s a blight devastated Bohemia's potato crop. Because many peasant families relied on the potato as a dietary staple, widespread hunger and even starvation followed. Still, many Czechs expressed great reluctance to leave their homeland in the early 1840s. Immigration overseas seemed a drastic solution to the famine, and many preferred to starve in their native land rather than abandon the soil their family had tilled for generations.

The revolutions of 1848 changed the Czechs' attitude about leaving home. The turmoil reinforced many intellectuals' determination to leave, and some peasants decided to follow their lead. By that time, reports from the approximately 500 political refugees who had already resettled in the United States had reached European Czechs, presenting a glowing picture of a country bursting with opportunity and laden with gold. By 1849 word of the gold strike at Sutter's Mill, California, aroused even greater interest in immigration to the United States. According to the February 14, 1848, edition of the Czech newspaper *Noviny Lípy Slovanské*:

> Reports continue to arrive from California concerning the large quantities of gold unearthed there. Nuggets of gold ore weighing as much as a pound, in some cases two, have been found. There are instances on record of emigrants making in gold digging and in trading with the Indians as much as $30,000. The average earnings of a person per day amount to $100. . . . A merchant's clerk commands $3,000 a year.

Other news of America came from the advertisements of shipping companies, which reaped enormous profits from the transportation of immigrants to North America.

*A cartoon from an Iowa City newspaper, printed in Czech, depicts life before and after immigration. Similar illustrations of prosperity in America filled Bohemian journals during the late 1800s and encouraged the exodus of Czechs from their native land.*

## The Long Journey

Despite these many enticements, most Czechs carefully weighed the advantages and disadvantages of emigrating. They viewed the decision to move as a grave one, in part because it meant uprooting their entire family. In many other immigrant groups, a family typically sent ahead one member, usually a young, single male, to the New World, with the idea that he would either make and save a great deal of money and return home or send for the rest of the family once he had established himself. By contrast, Czechs made the journey as a family and often regarded their stay in America as permanent.

*Although most Czech immigrants arrived in America before World War I, Czechs continued to set sail for the United States throughout the 20th century. Here two peasant women from Czechoslovakia pose on the deck of the SS Harding in 1939.*

The trip to the United States strained human tolerance for discomfort. Most Czechs began their ordeal by traveling from Bohemia to the German port cities of Hamburg and Bremen. From there ships sailed out into the North Sea and then headed west across the Atlantic, landing in New York City and, later, Galveston, Texas. Immigrants were herded into dank holds where they breathed fetid air and ate rotting food. Diseases spread like wildfire under such unwholesome conditions. In addition, immigrants often had to withstand abusive treatment from the ship's crew. According to Francis Dvornik, author of "Czech Contributions to the Growth of the United States":

> The food served to the immigrants was so coarse and unpalatable that young children could not digest it and cried with hunger. In addition, the drinking water doled out was barely sufficient to keep down the thirst of the people. There was none whatever for washing except salty sea water which was entirely unfit for that purpose. Looking back now it would seem unendurable, but we and the others stood it for seven long weeks until we reached New York.

The grueling trip grew shorter with the advent of the steam-powered ship, which gained wide usage in the latter half of the 19th century. By about 1900, passenger ships had transported more than 137,000 Czechs to the United States.

## A New Beginning

Once in America, immigrants had to withstand a battery of tests and inspections. Immigrants who arrived in New York Harbor before 1892 were processed at Castle Garden immigration station; those who arrived in later years went through Ellis Island. At these points of entry prospective residents had their bodies examined for disease, their finances scrutinized, and their names mangled by American inspectors. But for the immigrants America was the promised land, and to most of them the indignities suffered at Ellis Island constituted only minor deterrents.

After gaining entry, many Czechs tried to locate relatives who had preceded them to America. Those destined for the small Czech communities that had sprung up in New York City, Chicago, or St. Louis faced confusion and frustration. They roamed a vast network of urban thoroughfares, trying to match incomprehensible street signs to the scribbled address they held in their hand.

Those newcomers without prior connections in the United States often headed west. They usually traveled from New York to Albany by boat, from Albany to Buffalo by rail, from Buffalo to Chicago by boat, crossing over the Great Lakes with a stop in Detroit. All in all, the trip to Illinois from New York City lasted

*The Castle Garden immigration station, in New York City, as represented by American lithographer Nathaniel Currier in about 1848.*

*A poster advertises the availability
of cheap land in Iowa and
Nebraska. The prairie states of
the Midwest were anxious to
attract immigrant settlers.*

an average of five or six days. Initially, St. Louis attracted large numbers of Czechs who traveled up the
Mississippi River and, reaching the final port, settled
there. But when Chicago was connected to the East by
rail in 1853, it became cheaper and quicker to reach
Chicago and points west by train. Although New York
itself had a large and growing Czech population, Chicago was destined to become one of the largest Czech
cities in the world, second only to Prague.

Czechs were attracted to America's wide-open
spaces and the promise of owning their own acreage.
In the old country, Czechs traditionally kept a small
plot of land on which to grow vegetables for family
use, but only the gentry owned large tracts of prop-
erty. Thus, most Czechs equated land ownership with
wealth and aristocratic privilege, and they were willing
to travel far and wide by rail and ship in order to find
land to clear and cultivate.

In 1862 the lure of the West grew even stronger
when the U.S. Congress passed the Homestead Act,
which offered a 160-acre plot to anyone willing to live
on it and work it for a minimum of five years. Czechs
took advantage of this opportunity and moved by the
thousands to the wooded states of Wisconsin, Michigan, and Minnesota and the prairie states of Iowa, Nebraska, Kansas, and the Dakotas. They joined fellow
Czechs who had arrived earlier and established cities
with Czech names such as Pilsen, Prague, Slovan, and
Tabor. Czech families also moved into settlements
founded by other ethnic groups. So many converged
upon Milligan, Nebraska, that a town originally settled
by the Irish came to be known as a center of Czech
immigrants.

## Land of Their Own

The first farming town to be settled by Czechs was
Caledonia, Wisconsin, located north of Racine. Many
Czech pioneers arrived on foot, carrying feather beds
and a few cooking pots. To raise money for living ex-
penses, they leveled fields and sold the timber as fire-
wood. Czechs flocked to the wooded landscapes of the
Midwest for several reasons. When cut, wood pro-

vided both an instant building material and a ready source of income. Czechs used their profits from timber sales to buy farming equipment and other necessities. Woodland terrain usually offered an abundance of lakes and rivers and thus was easily accessible by boat, especially when compared with the inland prairies of the central United States. Finally, the woods of America reminded Czechs of their homeland. The cool, damp climate of states such as Michigan and Wisconsin resembled the weather back home.

*In 1933, V. F. Kučera (top row, left) posed with his family in Cheyenne County, Nebraska, where he founded a Czech colony near the town of Lodge Pole.*

Once they cleared the land, Czechs planted potatoes, wheat, fruit, and vegetables, and they kept dairy cows. The virgin prairies of Iowa, Nebraska, and Kansas yielded corn, wheat, and rye, crops well known to the Czech farmer. Grain production naturally led to the construction of breweries, and Czechs, who traditionally drink great quantities of beer, established several beer-making factories, of which two, Pilsen and Budweiser, continue to thrive.

The Czechs could afford to build these enterprises because they brought more money with them to the United States than did most other ethnic groups. According to immigration statistics from the turn of the century, the average Czech immigrant declared $23.12 upon arrival. In contrast, other newcomers had an average of only about $15.00. Czechs used their savings wisely, to fund their travel to the West and to finance their settlements and business ventures.

Whether they plowed the fields or manned breweries, most Czech immigrants of the 1850s congregated in Wisconsin. Wisconsin had been home to a large German community since the 1840s, and because many Czechs spoke German, they could function easily in and around the German settlements there. After the passage of the Homestead Act, Czechs settled farther and farther west. By 1900, the five states with the greatest Czech population were Illinois (with more than 77,000), Nebraska (with slightly fewer than 40,000), and Ohio, Wisconsin, and New York, each with a Czech population of about 30,000. Although Czechs had dispersed throughout the United States by

*Czech farmers thresh hay in Schuyler, Nebraska, in 1893.*

*A group of men in Wilber, Nebraska, stand in front of the local barbershop, a small business typical of those founded by Czech immigrants during their first decades in the United States. The photo was taken in about 1905.*

the turn of the century, they tended to land in large towns with Czech communities and stay there awhile before moving on to unknown territory.

Although Czechs tended to cluster in the Midwest, a sizeable community emerged in an unexpected state—Texas. Many from the initial wave of Czech migration in the 1850s were drawn to Texas by two Moravian pastors, Ernst Bergman and Joseph Zvolánek. These churchmen convinced many of their former congregants to come to Texas by writing them letters and urging them to immigrate. Those persuaded to migrate usually traveled from Germany to Galveston by boat and then settled in either Galveston, Houston, or nearby regions.

## A Shifting Population

Most Czech immigrants of the mid-1800s knew no life other than farming, and they delighted in the free land available to them. Nevertheless, many Czechs suffered from the isolation of rural life in America. Accustomed to small villages, they greatly missed the close communities of small-town Bohemia. Their yearning for Czech culture was eased a bit with the arrival of increasing numbers of their compatriots during the latter part of the 19th century.

*In small American towns such as New Prague, Minnesota, Czechs in the New World tried to re-create the village life they had known at home.*

In 1873 a severe economic depression hit Bohemia and triggered a new wave of Czech migration. Sugar-beet farmers were particularly hard hit by the crisis. European agriculture continued to suffer into the 1880s and 1890s. As a result, many Bohemian farmers swarmed into the cities of their homeland to seek industrial work. This migration from the farm to the city transformed the Czech populace and similarly altered the profile of the typical Czech immigrant to America.

After 1890 the vast majority of Czech immigrants—who had once hailed from the countryside of Bohemia—now came from more urbanized areas. Czechs such as these composed the greatest single wave of Czech immigration to the United States: Between 1900 and 1910, 95,516 arrived on U.S. shores. Whereas their predecessors possessed considerable expertise in the cultivation of crops and the raising of dairy cows, urban Czech immigrants knew the life of the factory. They found employment as skilled workers in cigar factories and in the garment industry. By 1900, 45 percent of foreign-born Czechs in the United States lived in urban areas such as New York, Cleveland, and Chicago, with the Windy City claiming more Czech residents than New York and Cleveland combined.

Although Czechs were used to urban life, many nevertheless settled on the outskirts of the city, where they could breathe fresh air and still benefit from the increased opportunities available to them in an urban center. A study of Czech Americans living in Cleveland in 1919, for example, found that none lived in the most congested urban neighborhoods but noted that

Czechs abounded "on the edge of the city where town and country meet; when the city follows they move on. The older Czech still loves his own fenced-in yard, where he can have a vegetable garden, some bright colored flowers, and a few ducks and geese."

## The New Immigrants: Refugees and Political Exiles

The movement of Czech immigrants from farm to factory and from country to city to suburb reflected changes occurring in America as a whole. As the 19th century gave way to the 20th, America found that it no longer required the huge labor force that had been arriving each year from Europe. U.S. lawmakers began closing the golden door to the land of opportunity. In 1924, Congress passed the Johnson-Reed Act, the first permanent quota that restricted the legal entry of immigrants into the United States. Three years later a national origins plan, which limited the entire number of European immigrants entering the United States, was put into effect. The 1927 law fixed quotas for in-

*Young girls work in a cigar factory in about 1905. Although the work could be dirty and tedious, many Czech women took jobs in cigar factories.*

dividual countries at one-sixth of one percent of the number of people of that heritage living in the United States at the time of the 1920 census. The law thus gave preference to emigrants from northern and western Europe, whose descendants had by now grown to a sizable population in America. Czechs, from central Europe, were not adversely affected by the quota laws. They had come to America relatively early, in the mid-19th century, and hence were able to continue immigrating well into the middle of the 20th century, when the quota laws were rewritten.

Czech immigration to the United States from about 1938 to the early 1950s was spurred by the fear of Nazism and, in the postwar era, communism. In the late 1930s several hundred Jewish Czechs fled Czechoslovakia to escape the Nazi occupation. During and after the war very few Czechs had the chance to immigrate

*The Winn family emigrated from Czechoslovakia on the eve of World War II. They are shown here in their New York apartment in 1942 as they eat dinner in a family dining room decorated with a framed picture of Tomáš Masaryk.*

In 1969, Czech seaman Jiri Vokrouhlik jumped ship in Los Angeles harbor and swam ashore to seek political asylum. After World War II, many Czechs opposed to their nation's communist government attempted to come to the United States.

to the United States, but in 1949 immigration increased again when the Communist party took over in Czechoslovakia and began arresting and imprisoning those it deemed its enemies. In the same year the U.S. Congress passed the Displaced Persons Act, which allowed approximately 205,000 Europeans displaced by the upheaval created by World War II to enter. This liberalization of the immigration law enabled about 25,000 Czech refugees and political exiles to find asylum in the United States.

The immigrants of the 1940s included many professional and highly skilled workers. They differed from most Czech Americans in their level of education and in the fact that they immigrated by necessity rather than choice. Yet these 20th-century Czech immigrants shared the common language, culture, and traditions that have bound Czech Americans together ever since they began settling towns and cities across America.

*The Zeleny Cash Store, shown here in 1911, was founded by a Czech immigrant in Hutchinson, Minnesota.*

# WHERE CITY AND COUNTRY MEET

Czechs who arrived in the United States after 1890 enjoyed two advantages unusual for Slavic immigrants. They were skilled workers—proficient as butchers, carpenters, tailors, blacksmiths, or cigar makers—and they could read and write in their native tongue. Because Czechs had always held formal education in high regard, on the whole they were much more literate than other Slavic groups. About 97 percent of Czech immigrants could read and write, whereas the general literacy rate among Slavs averaged only 66 percent.

In the New World the differences between Czechs and other Slavs surfaced most dramatically in the type of work they chose. According to Tomas Čapek, author of *The Čechs in America*, immigrants from Bohemia and Moravia rarely worked in unskilled outdoor labor—such as road building or bricklaying—or in mining. By contrast, immigrants from Slovakia provided the work force for the coal mines and steel mills of Pennsylvania. Whether Czech Americans set out for the plains or settled in cities—as did most of those who arrived after 1890—the challenges were the same: The immigrant and his or her family had to find a means of financial support, a place to live, and a community of fellow Czechs who might offer advice, comfort, and company. Although they possessed many skills, Czechs soon discovered that their abilities did not always guarantee them immediate employment. The big

*Many Czech immigrants were skilled workers who either gained ready acceptance into America's labor force or established independent businesses. J. J. Havlovic started this blacksmith shop in Wilber, Nebraska.*

cities of America housed huge populations of immigrants, many of whom had once been the one master carpenter or blacksmith back home. Suddenly these people found themselves thrown together and competing for the same few jobs. In order to survive, many had to enter fields of employment that were new to them but that at least offered a chance to earn a living.

Like other 19th-century ethnic groups, the Czechs tended to work together in businesses founded by their countrymen. The vast majority found employment as garment workers or cigar makers, two industries dominated by Czech immigrants. The history of Czechs in the cigar industry dates back to the days of the Hapsburg Empire. In the late 19th century the tobacco industry in Austria functioned as a government monopoly. The Bohemian town of Sedlec contained one of the largest cigar factories within Austrian-controlled territory, an establishment that employed more than 2,000 workers.

In the 1860s several of these workers emigrated to New York City to ply their trade there. They soon encouraged others from Sedlec to join them in America and benefit from the substantially higher wages offered in the United States. According to one estimate, by 1873 about 95 percent of all Czech New Yorkers worked in the cigar-making industry. When factory jobs were scarce, Czechs worked at home doing the often dirty and smelly chore of stripping leaves and rolling cigars. Frequently, the whole family joined in. Children were kept out of school to help the family earn enough to live on. In 1888 the New York legislature abolished home cigar making, so many young Czechs set out for the factories. An article in the December 3, 1904, edition of the magazine *Charities* described a typical cigar factory:

> The Bohemian girls dread going into the cigar factories. The hygiene is bad, the moral influences are often not the best, and the work is exhausting. . . . The strippers and bookmakers who get the tobacco ready for the cigarmakers work together—sometimes as many as a hundred and fifty of them—at the end of a room laden with tobacco dust and heavy with the odor of damp tobacco leaves. The windows are generally kept closed because the tobacco must not be allowed to become dry.

*Czech cigar makers roll cigars at home, in a photograph by American photographer and social reformer Jacob Riis.*

Those Czechs not engaged in cigar making often worked to manufacture mother-of-pearl buttons, a popular decorative item for women's blouses during the 1800s. In *The Čechs in America,* Tomas Čapek traces the lineage of this industry in America to about 1890, when several pearl-button makers came to the United States from Žirovnice, a provincial Bohemian town famed for the production of pearl buttons. The Žirovnice workers introduced their craft to the United States, and by 1920 three-quarters of all pearl buttons were manufactured by about 50 small, Czech-owned factories in the East.

Although Czechs as a group succeeded in finding a niche in American industry, many individuals still had difficulty obtaining employment. In *The Čechs in America,* author Vera Laska tells the story of Frank Brodsky, a Czech Jew, who searched for a job for a long time:

> He was reduced to such want that he could not even buy a second-hand pair of shoes. Ashamed to have to walk barefoot, he blackened his feet every morning with shoeblack in order to give the impression that he had shoes on and continued his search on New York streets. At last he found a job on a whale boat. He made a new start with a few dollars he saved. Then returning to New York he eventually became a wealthy man.

## Rural Life

Czech immigrants whose specialized training was not sufficient to win them jobs in the cities found themselves moving west and settling in farm country, in communities established by earlier migrations of Czechs to America. Thousands of Czech immigrants left the cities of the Northeast with the hope of acquiring land, a house, and economic independence. Their skills were put to the test on 100-acre farms, which required an able hand and a great deal of patience. Managing a large farm was a new challenge, and poor soil, drought, and periodic grasshopper plagues made the trial even tougher.

*(continued on page 73)*

*Overleaf: The grave of this Czech immigrant in St. Michael's Cemetery in New York City reflects his dual heritage as a Czech and an American. The epitaph on the tombstone is written in Czech.*

*Czechs in America and the old country take pride in the adage "If he's Czech, he's a musician." At left, the Czech Heritage Band plays at the village bandstand in Cedar Rapids, Iowa. The group performs authentic arrangements similar to those popularized by traditional bands in the Czech Republic's capital city of Prague (above).*

The setting may change, but the delight Czechs take in their traditional dances remains a constant. At left, Czech dancers perform "Moldoveaskaya," a Moravian folk dance, on New York City's Wall Street during a festival held to promote ethnic pride. The dancers' costumes are modeled after traditional garb from their homeland (above).

*Pedestrians in Prague (right) cross the Charles IV Bridge, named for the Bohemian monarch who was crowned Holy Roman Emperor in 1355 and won fame for his patronage of the arts and education. Many Czech Americans, such as this group at the Czech Village in Cedar Rapids, Iowa (below), are dedicated to preserving the rich history of Czechs in North America and Europe.*

In the United States, time-honored Czech crafts underwent permutations reflecting the American experience of immigrant artisans. The traditional clock at left was carved by the Billy brothers, Czech immigrants whose work is preserved in a museum in Spillville, Iowa. Its interior is filled with handcarved wooden figurines of American presidents and other personages. By the latter half of the 20th century, North American culture had permeated the old country as well: In Prague in the mid-1980s (above), a teenager looks at a display in a record store that features American singers Madonna and Stevie Wonder alongside Czech entertainers.

*(continued from page 64)*

In Texas, most Czechs first worked as tenant farmers, tilling land owned by another person and paying rent for their own small plots either in cash or produce. Within a few years the majority of Czech immigrants amassed enough savings to buy their own land, animals, tools, and seed. Czechs in Texas, as in the Midwest, fought a brave battle against the blights that constantly threatened to ruin their cotton crops. Insects often devastated a field of cotton in a single day. If the crop survived these pests, it rarely escaped damage from the elements: hailstorms, droughts, and flooding all plagued farmers, often bringing them to ruin. Yet in America, Czechs earned a reputation as diligent and capable farmers who could grow crops on land others had given up on.

On the Great Plains many Czech pioneers lacked lumber for building and literally had to carve out sod houses to live in, as described by an early Czech settler:

*Two farmers of Czech descent pose in front of their home near Black River Falls, Wisconsin, in 1937. Wisconsin remains home to a large Czech community.*

> Father dug a hole in a hill on land bought from the government at one dollar and twenty-five cents per acre. Over the hole, which was about 10 x 12 feet, father built our home. He arranged logs on the four sides with three beams for girders to hold the dirt roof. There was a door and one window on one end.

*A family of Czech Americans gather in the fields around their farm in Waskich, Minnesota, in about 1900.*

Czech women took great pains to beautify their homes, however humble. Dirt walls were smoothed and whitened with plaster, and feather beds were tucked into hollows in the wall for extra warmth and insulation. As soon as possible, families moved from sod dwellings into actual farmhouses.

## Music and Dance

Czechs in the Midwest went to great lengths to socialize with compatriots living in nearby territories. In rural America they worked hard to build a community and to keep alive the traditions of music and dance that had always been an important aspect of life in Bohemia.

Music filled the lives of Czech Americans, who took pride in the old saying *Co Čech to muzikant*, meaning "If he's a Czech, he's a musician." The musical traditions of Bohemia encompassed a wide range of styles, from polkas to the hundreds of hymns and chants that Czechs, especially those belonging to the Moravian Brethren, sang in church ceremonies. This sacred music proved to be a vital influence on Czech composer Antonín Dvořák, who was invited to America in 1892 to direct New York's National Conservatory of Music, an institution devoted to the development of American music and opera. During his three years in New York, Dvořák grew to love American folk music, which he began incorporating into his compositons. In 1893 he spent a summer in the small Czech community of Spillville, Iowa, where he wrote his Symphony in E Minor (From the New World), a musical portrayal of life in America. This piece gained great popularity among Czech Americans because it synthesized elements of Old World and New World music.

Evidence of the important place music occupied in the life of Czech Americans may be found in Willa Cather's novel of Czech life on the prairie, *My Ántonia*. In this classic work of American literature, an ancient but cherished violin brought to America by Ántonia Shimerda's father symbolizes the determination of the Czechs to preserve their traditions in the harsh yet beautiful new environment in which they found themselves. Mr. Shimerda's refusal to play his violin, perhaps his most prized possession, serves to illustrate the depths of his longing for the homeland he has left behind, as Ántonia relates in the passage that follows. Ultimately, his despair leads him to commit suicide.

*Czech composer Antonín Dvořák posed for this photograph in 1893, during his stay in Iowa. His* From the New World *symphony, written during that time, conveys his impressions of American life.*

> My Papa sad for the old country. He not look good. He never make music any more. At home he play violin all the time; for weddings and for dance. Here never. When I beg him for play, he shake his head no. Some days he take his violin out of his box and make with his fingers on the strings, like this, but never he make the music. He don't like this kawn-tree.

Czechs frequently traveled miles to listen to the lively tunes of their native land, played by fellow farmers or traveling musicians. Polkas were particular favorites. Invented by a Czech band to honor the Polish people, polkas achieved great popularity in America. Although originally quite simple, polka dance steps became increasingly elaborate and the province of professional dancers. The catchy rhythm of the polka sparked a craze that swept America in the late 1800s.

Czech bands made regular and welcome appearances at traditional weddings. The Czech wedding has been described as "a virtual orgy of eating, drinking, dancing, and visiting." A typical wedding required months, if not a full year, of planning. The bride's family raised additional chickens, turkeys, geese, and an extra calf and hog, which were all roasted to perfection and served at a banquet following the ceremony. Women from the community spent several days preparing such beloved Bohemian dishes as *zapečené vepřovi* (cooked pork), *domácí chleba* (homemade bread), *kyselé zelí* (sauerkraut), and *pečivo* (pastries). Villagers

*In 1914, Victoria Novak and Louis Hanska, a bride and groom of Czech descent, eschewed traditional Czech wedding attire in favor of more modern garb.*

seized the opportunity to don their finest clothing, worn only on special occasions. Women stepped into brightly colored skirts, which they topped with an embroidered blouse and a vest trimmed in black with gold or lace. Men generally wore vests of comparable splendor.

Both in the city and in the country Czech traditions survived and helped bind Czechs together into a united ethnic group. Music, the sharing of food and drink, and the day-to-day exchange of goods and gossip helped preserve the language and the traditional way of life. But Czechs of the first and second generation yearned to do more than preserve their people's time-honored customs in the New World. Many Czechs born in the United States—or those who had spent several decades there—tried to integrate their unique traditions with those of their adopted country. Younger Czechs looked for avenues into the mainstream of American life, and many discovered a path in the field of politics.

## The Political Realm

Urban Czechs soon discovered that many of the most important political positions had already been filled by the Irish, who had preceded the Czechs to the United States. Therefore, most 19th-century Czechs with political ambitions tried to make a name for themselves in the small towns of less populated states—Michigan, Nebraska, and Wisconsin, for example—that most Czechs inhabited. Once elected, a politician could see to the needs of the constituency, including his or her own ethnic group, and could initiate campaigns for better housing, education, and legislation favorable to the usually disadvantaged immigrants.

One pioneer lawmaker of Czech origin was Augustin Haidusek, one of the most influential Czech Americans in Texas. Born in Moravia in 1845, Haidusek journeyed to Galveston, Texas, with his parents in October 1856. He spent his early years in America on a farm, remaining there until he joined the Confederate army in 1863. After the Civil War, Haidusek taught school and began to study law. In 1870 he became the first Czech Texan to earn a legal degree. Five years later Haidusek won a mayoral election in La Grange, Texas, and he quickly advanced from that municipal post to service in the Texas legislature. In the following decade he returned to local politics, as Fayette County judge. Haidusek died in 1928.

The roster of Czech politicians also includes Edward Rosewater, who served in the Nebraska state legislature in 1870–71; Adolph Sabath, a U.S. congressman from Chicago who represented his constituency from 1907 to 1952; and Anton Čermák. In 1931, Čermák was elected mayor of Chicago, but his term of office ended prematurely two years later when he was slain by an assassin who had intended to kill President Franklin Roosevelt, who was then visiting Chicago.

Czech Americans contributed to mainstream party politics, but their greatest achievement resulted from their skill as organizers for the Socialist Labor party. Socialism developed as a political ideology in Europe in the mid-19th century in response to the drastic changes in the continent's economy caused by the Industrial Revolution, which was drawing millions of farmers away from the land and into the bleak factories

*Chicago mayor Anton Čermák stands alongside a new automobile made by Nash Motors. Čermák was one of the most prominent Czech-American politicians.*

springing up in Europe's cities. Men, women, and children—such as those who labored at the Sedlec, Bohemia, cigar factory—toiled endless hours under unsafe and unhealthy conditions in exchange for exploitative wages. Socialists worked to end these inequities and devoted themselves to organizing factory workers into labor unions.

In 1866, Czech-American socialists organized their first political club. Six years later they banded together to form a trade union for New York City cigar makers. In 1878 the Czech labor movement, represented by Leo Meilbek, won a seat in the Illinois state legislature. Czech-American socialists played an integral role in the political campaigns of Eugene V. Debs, who ran for the presidency on the Socialist ticket five times after 1900.

## Education

Just as they plunged into U.S. politics, so too Czech Americans became active in the field of education. In smaller towns, especially on the frontier or in closeknit Czech communities, Czech Americans often decided which teachers were hired in the local schools and which subjects were taught there. Czechs expressed a great desire for their children to learn about Czech literature and history, subjects not usually taught in public schools.

In fact, Czechs so greatly valued education that they established many language schools, religious schools, and even a college. In 1855, Czech Catholics established the first Czech-language school, in St. Louis, Missouri. By 1930 approximately 21,000 Czech Americans attended 121 parochial elementary schools and 1 high school founded by Czech Catholics in the United States. Czechs in Illinois founded a college, the Benedictines' College of St. Procopius at Lisle, Illinois, site of a Czech-Catholic abbey. The school served as a seminary to prepare Czech and Slovak boys for the priesthood. Teachers and students there generally spoke both Czech and English. (Today, under the new name of Benedictine University, the school offers a liberal arts curriculum for both men and women.) By founding schools that pro-

*The main building of Benedictine University, which was founded in Lisle, Illinois, in 1887 to provide Czech-speaking Catholic priests for the large Czech Catholic community in Chicago.*

moted Czech culture, Czech Americans contributed to the preservation of their heritage in North America.

It took more than a few classes in Czech history and language to convey the everyday aspects of being a member of a special group. Czechs preserved their traditional culture in the home as well, with Czech books, ornaments, and pictures from the old country. In general, those from poorer families maintained a Czech identity longer than more affluent Czechs, who strove for acceptance in middle-class America. Indeed, the Czech community included a broad cross section of middle-class and poor people; Protestants and Catholics; urban dwellers and rural farmers; intellectuals and laborers; socialists and conservatives. The majority of Czechs, no matter what their family background, lived in tight-knit enclaves in several American towns and cities. Three of the most well known of these Czech-American communities were Chicago, Illinois; Milligan, Nebraska; and Bohemia, New York.

## "Czech-ago"

During the late 19th century, so many Czechs resided in Chicago that longtime residents nicknamed their city "Czech-ago." The Windy City received its first Czech immigrants in 1852; by 1870 that number had increased to 6,300. Most men and women there found work as skilled tailors in the city's garment industry. It did not take long for the Czech neighborhoods in the city to become practically self-sufficient. In the business district Czech banks, stores, cafes, and res-

*Members of the First Czechoslovak Garden Club of America pose in Chicago in 1935. Many Czech-American organizations had their headquarters in Chicago, which is still home to the largest community of Czechs in the United States.*

taurants lined the streets. In some Czech areas, such as the "Prague" settlement, it was possible to carry on business using the Czech language exclusively, much to the surprise and delight of newcomers.

By 1920 Czechs in Chicago numbered some 200,000, including both the first and second generations. Rather than working in large factories, as in New York, they tended to work in offices, garment shops, and their own small businesses. Chicago Czechs prospered. Many could afford to move out of the center of the city and buy larger plots of land where they could live in bigger houses and even grow small gardens. Typical Czech homes in Chicago were cottages with a small plot of grass in front and a garden in the back. Houses were unattached for greater privacy, with a narrow walk or alley between neighboring buildings. Generally, Czechs were comfortable in the same types of houses that other Americans lived in; their only request was that there be room in the yard for a garden. Most Czechs moved to the south and west of Chicago proper, thus expanding the city limits in those directions.

Chicago Czechs owned grocery stores, banks, and real estate offices. By 1924 they controlled 15 state and federal banks in Chicago and over 50 percent of the assets of all building and loan associations in the city.

Chicago was also the center of a thriving mail-order business in products made in Czechoslovakia such as books, glassware, hops and malt for brewing beer, stationery, pictures, toys, and ornaments. Chicago is still home to the largest concentration of Americans of Czech descent in the United States, and it remains a hub of Czech culture.

## Milligan, Nebraska

Milligan might be considered Chicago's rural counterpart. In 1930, 1,100 people lived in Milligan; 9 out of 10 of those claimed Czech heritage. The town hall, the largest building on Main Street, served as the center of social activity in town. People came from far and near to attend dances and other gatherings there, as described in *Story of a Bohemian-American Village* by Robert Kutak:

> "Open nights" were social events where farmers came to town to patronize stores which stayed open for this special occasion. On these evenings the brightly lighted store windows of Main Street look out upon a busy throng of men, women, and children, hurrying from one place to another, buying prodigious amounts of food and clothing. On the street outside the storefronts fat rosy-cheeked farmer wives stand and gossip, while their children play. . . . The men of the family gather at Central Hall to play cards and discuss the crops and the economic situation. On Main Street farmers meet and hire harvest hands.

*Czech-American residents of the town of Wilber, Nebraska, stand inside the Kunc meat market, producer of gustatory delights known locally as Wilber Wieners.*

These social gatherings still present Milligan residents with a chance to get together after days of working on the farm, away from the company of neighbors. On Sundays in particular, Czechs spent their afternoons visiting, relaxing, and gossiping with one another. Women got together and talked about friends and relatives; men could be found loafing on benches lining Main Street. On winter evenings women gathered to quilt or strip feathers for feather beds.

The intimacy of small-town life, although not unique to Milligan, was rare in more urban Czech communities. Czechs who wanted to reside near an urban center yet still maintain the spirit of the Bohemian village found a good mixture of city and country in the New York suburb of Bohemia, Long Island.

## Bohemia, Long Island

In 1857, members of the Koula, Vavra, and Kratochvil families settled the Long Island town known today as Bohemia. These newcomers to America moved to Long Island after spending several years working in the crowded cigar factories of New York City. Several other families soon joined them, and together they tried to build an old Bohemian town on American soil. Although only 60 miles from New York City, the area was densely wooded and abundant with deer.

In the early days of settlement, the simple act of visiting a neighbor, a favorite Czech pastime, could be quite a problem. According to a history of the area, printed by the Bohemia Historical Society,

> Surrounded by woodland without roads or paths, each family had to get bearings on the other by climbing a tall tree, looking for the mark each had placed there; a long stick. Taking a sight upon this, the husband would point out the direction, and his wife would start toward their objective. The husband would follow after reaching the ground from his observation point—having made sure his wife was continuing in the right direction.

At night navigation from one household to another presented even more of a problem, and settlers used pine pitch torches to light the way.

At first families in Bohemia managed to be self-sufficient, but within a few years many found that they needed a regular source of income to purchase necessities. Some secured employment on the estates dotting Long Island's wealthy South Shore. Those types of jobs proved too few to support the whole community, so Bohemia residents turned to the industries most familiar to them, cigar and button making. At first, Czechs living in Bohemia manufactured cigars in their homes, but several of the town's wealthier members built factories, thereby providing employment for hundreds of villagers.

In 1890 the Bohemia branch of the Czecho-Slovak Protective Society, a nationwide organization, inaugurated a movement to build a monument to Czech patriot Jan Hus. Unveiled three years later, the statue of Hus was one of the first memorials ever erected in America to honor a foreigner.

## Keeping History Alive

In 1995, President Bill Clinton and the presidents of both the Czech and Slovak republics attended the dedication of a $2.6 million building to house the expanding collection of the National Czech and Slovak Museum and Library in Cedar Rapids, Iowa. Founded in 1974 as a celebration of the vibrant Czech legacy in Cedar Rapids—stretching back to the 1850s—it has grown to hold the largest collection of Czech and Slovak materials outside the home republics.

The museum houses some 5,000 artifacts up to 400 years old, and the library serves as a repository for geographical information and genealogical research. Not content to serve only the local Czech population, the museum organizes exhibits that tour the country.

*The Czech-American residents of Bohemia, New York, erected this monument to Jan Hus in 1890.*

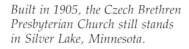
*Built in 1905, the Czech Brethren Presbyterian Church still stands in Silver Lake, Minnesota.*

# RELIGION AND COMMUNITY

O nce the Czechs had established themselves in rural towns and urban ethnic neighborhoods, they began to look beyond the challenge of daily survival. Czech Americans of the early 1900s enriched their lives with active membership in fraternal societies, sokols, and church groups. Most Czech-American community activity had a particular ideological bent: Catholics, socialists, freethinkers, and intellectuals banded together in their own groups. Yet the major division was between those who practiced Catholicism and those who did not.

## The Church in Czech Life

Many Czechs associated the Roman Catholic church with the long history of political and cultural repression in their homeland. They equated the church with the Hapsburg Empire and the empire's repression of the Protestant religion. According to historian Karen Johnson Freeze, the Czechs "had bitter memories of the Catholic church as a militant arm of the state. . . . Most Czechs associated it and its representatives with the German language, German oppression, and German Hapsburg rulers." During the Hapsburg campaign to re-Catholicize Bohemia, many Czech peasants had been forced to demonstrate their allegiance to the

*Czech Catholics from Saunders County, Nebraska, pose for a group photograph with their priest in 1932.*

Roman Catholic church. They complied, but their hearts were not in it.

After they left Hapsburg-controlled territory, thousands of Czech immigrants bade farewell also to the Catholic church. In the United States approximately one-third to one-half of all Czechs ceased to practice Catholicism. Yet not all Czechs renounced their faith. In America, many joined the congregations of other European Catholics, including the Irish, the Germans, and the Polish.

The Czechs felt more positive about Protestantism. Their enthusiasm derived not only from strong belief in Protestant doctrine but also from a great reverence for all that Protestantism had stood for in Bohemia: patriotism, freedom from German rule, democracy, and the legitimization of Czech language and culture. Czech Protestants include among their ranks the descendants of the Hussites and the Moravian Brethren as well as Presbyterians, Episcopalians, and many other sects. The Jan Hus Presbyterian Church in New York City, founded in about 1888, is one of the most well-known Czech-Protestant congregations in the United States.

Many other Czech Americans took great pride in the legacy of Jan Hus but rejected Christianity in general. These men and women usually identified themselves as members of one of three active nonreligious

Czech groups: freethinkers, socialists, or atheists. The freethinkers movement originated in Bohemia in the 1870s and was essentially a radical anti-Hapsburg and antichurch organization. Freethinkers believed that people should be guided by reason rather than faith. They wrote a 14-point creed, established free-thought schools, and even created original rites and ceremonies for marriages, funerals, and other important events.

In the homeland most Czech freethinkers had respected the right of Catholics to worship as they chose, as long as they did not impose their religious views upon other people. But when Czech freethinkers settled in America, they remembered well the abuses of the Catholic church within the Hapsburg Empire. In their new country, the freethinkers vehemently opposed any consolidation of power by the Roman Catholic church. They were joined in their opposition to the church by Czech socialists and atheists, two other groups central to the Czech community.

Despite the Czech tendency to reject organized religion, Catholicism and Protestantism continued to claim many Czech adherents in America. Czech Catholics built their first American church, St. Jan Nepomuk, in St. Louis in 1854, and Czech-Catholic parishes proliferated between 1860 and 1880. Czech Catholics built their first church in Chicago, the center of the Czech community in America, in 1864. By 1920 about 350 Czech priests served congregants in 268 Czech parishes, the greatest number of which, 68 in all, were located in Texas. Although fewer in number, Czech-Protestant churches also attracted thousands of newcomers. Most Czechs belonged to the Presbyterian sect of the religion, which claimed 3,500 Czech followers by 1920. During the same time Texas alone had 24 parishes with a total of 1,500 members—all belonging to the Unity of Bohemian-Moravian Brethren.

## The Czech Press

The various factions within Czech settlements in the New World found their views well represented by a vigorous partisan press. Newspapers sympathetic to either the Christian, socialist, or freethinker philoso-

*The Bohemian Reading and Educational Society, founded by freethinkers in about 1915, was located between the Minnesota towns of Silver Lake and Hutchinson.*

phies provided a steady supply of community news mixed with editorials either praising or condemning some aspect of the Czech community. In fact, Czech-American journalists commanded more power within the community than any other single group. According to Tomas Čapek:

> . . . the [newspaper] editor not only wrote for the people, he literally thought for them. His advice on matters relating to the affairs of the community never failed to command attention. . . . The editor was invariably picked out to umpire quarrels, many of which, by the way, were of his own making. He was chosen as orator to address meetings and conventions, played leading roles at amateur theatricals, taught the local Czech language school, helped to organize new lodges, was called upon to write funeral orations, political speeches, and banquet toasts.

*The August 20, 1892, issue of* Svoboda, *a Czech-language newspaper, covered the Democratic convention of that year.*

Czech journalists displayed great energy in leading the community and in launching new publications. Between 1860 and 1910, Czech Americans founded approximately 326 newspapers. By 1920 only a fraction of these survived. Nevertheless, Czech-language periodicals today include over half a dozen daily newspapers, plus numerous newsletters written for local Czech communities.

Each interest group supported its own periodicals. Catholics subscribed to Father Joseph Molitor's *Katolické Noviny* (Catholic News), Father Hessoun's *Hlas* (Voice), or the Benedictine publications *Katolík* and *Národ* (the Nation). Socialists read *Dělnické listy* (Worker's Gazette), *Spravedlnost* (Justice), and others. Freethinkers subscribed to a wide range of newspapers, some of which dramatized in rich detail the "threat" posed by the Czech clergy in America. The most lurid of these, *Pokrok*, presented stories of lascivious priests and sinful nuns. The Czech press also printed a variety of newsletters and gazettes for the community's many special interest groups: Feminists, agricultural experts, and even poultry farmers were served by their own publications.

Among the most famous Czech-American editors was Charles Jonáš, who published one of the first Czech-American newspapers, *Slavie*, based in Racine, Wisconsin. *Slavie* was the result of a merger between the first two Czech-language dailies in America. In 1860, *Slován Amerikanskáy* (American Slav), based in Racine, and *Národní Noviny* (Nationalist Gazette), based in St. Louis, Missouri, began publication within one month of each other. By their first anniversary the two papers faced grave financial difficulties, and they decided to join forces rather than go out of business. In 1861 the first issue of *Slavie*, based in Racine, rolled off the presses; the paper remained in print until 1946.

Charles Jonáš was a Czech immigrant. Born in Bohemia in 1840, Jonáš established a reputation as a passionate student nationalist in his homeland. In 1863 he fled Bohemia to escape arrest and lived in London for several months. During that time he was asked to assume the helm at *Slavie*, where he remained for more

*A studio portrait taken in Racine, Wisconsin, shows newspaper publisher Charles Jonáš as a young man.*

than a decade. During Jonáš's tenure the paper achieved considerable prominence and became known for its steadfast and enthusiastic support for the candidates and platform of the Democratic party. In 1883, Jonáš began a second career and entered politics. During the next 11 years he served as state senator, consul to Prague, lieutenant governor of Wisconsin, and consul to St. Petersburg. Jonáš remained active until his death in 1896. He was buried in Prague, in accordance with his last wishes.

## Fraternal and Benevolent Societies

The division of the Czech-American press into Catholic and non-Catholic sectors corresponded to divisions in other areas of Czech life. For example, fraternal and benevolent societies—two important fixtures of the community—either sought or avoided a church affiliation. In fact, as late as 1978, one expert in Czech history discovered an Oklahoma lodge founded by a freethinking society and one established by a Catholic society only five miles apart, yet the members of these two groups hardly socialized with one another.

Although divided by affiliation and membership, fraternal and benevolent societies were united in a common purpose. They sought to preserve old World values and to act as a safety net to families who had lost their primary breadwinner to illness, death, or unemployment. In the early 20th century, when such economic cushions as social security, unemployment insurance, health insurance, and pensions were unknown in the American workplace, fraternal societies shouldered many responsibilities now borne by private companies or the U.S. government.

In 1854, Czech freethinkers established the first Czech-American fraternal society, the Českoslovanská Podporující Společnost (Czech-Slavonic Benevolent Society), known commonly as the CSPS. The CSPS sponsored many cultural and social activities for the Czech community both in St. Louis and in remote towns throughout the Midwest. CSPS members built lodges in which they held dances and concerts and

*A plaque displays the membership of a Czech fraternal society in Iowa as it looked in 1882.*

performed plays. In 1883 the CSPS moved its headquarters to Chicago in recognition of that city's importance to Czech Americans. The Catholic equivalent of the freethinking CSPS was the Catholic Central Union, established in St. Louis in 1879.

At first the fraternal societies were the exclusive domain of men. The lodges adopted a military style—members attained different ranks, for example—and appealed to younger members by organizing parades and marches. As the years progressed, younger members were interested less in the cultural aspects of fraternal societies than in the economic security they offered. Women, too, wanted the benefit of fraternal

*Czech-American women wearing traditional Bohemian garb in 1938.*

organizations, but many societies refused to admit female members. In response to their exclusion, Czech women banded together and formed independent associations such as the Union of Czech Women, organized in 1870. By 1920 female membership in the Union had reached 20,000, more than all the other women's societies combined.

By the 1920s more than 2,500 Czech-American fraternal lodges, clubs, and societies had sprung up across America. Today these organizations are grouped under several major societies, including the Czechoslovak Society of America (formerly the CSPS). The Catholic lodges were united in 1889 into the Czech Catholic Union of Texas (now known simply as the Catholic Union of Texas). Given the history of division between Catholic and non-Catholic Czechs, it is not surprising that two of the largest fraternal societies still function independently of each other.

Many Czechs—even those without affiliation to a fraternal society—have lent their support to two other Czech-American organizations: the Czechoslovak National Council of America and the Czechoslovak Christian Democracy. Each of these groups exists to inform the American public about political and social affairs in the Czech Republic and Slovakia. Founded in 1918, the Czechoslovak National Council of America has long acted as a monitor of human rights issues in the Czech and Slovak homelands. The Czechoslovak Christian Democracy, established by Czech Americans in 1957 to help Czech refugees immigrate to and resettle in the United States, acts today as a link between the Czech community and the American people at large.

## Sokols

Czech Americans have joined together not only in fraternal societies but also in sokols, Czech gymnastic societies. The idea of the sokol (a Slavic word for falcon) originated in Prague in 1862. Freethinkers of that era established sokols in order to help people discipline their body and develop moral character and intelligence—two ideals of the free-thought movement. The father of the sokol movement, Dr. Miroslav Tyrs, wanted to create an organization that would not only promote physical fitness but instill in Czechs a national pride frequently denied them by the Hapsburg regime.

Eager to foster the feeling of shared identity and national and individual pride that had developed within the sokols, Czech immigrants were quick to es-

*Young Czech-American members of a sokol in Cadott, Wisconsin, demonstrate their grace and agility in this 1931 photograph.*

tablish their own gymnastic societies. In 1878, Czechs formed the National Sokol Union, which by 1985 included 48 branches across the United States. The movement reached its peak in 1927, when it claimed 125 branches and 14,000 members. About 6,500 of those enrolled in a sokol had achieved some degree of expertise in gymnastics. In 1879 the National Sokol Union held its first gymnastics festival (*slet*). Rather than highlight individual gymnasts, the performances featured a simultaneous performance by an ensemble that moved in time to music. Thus each member was able to take pride in both individual and group accomplishment—an ideal of the sokol philosophy.

## Folkways

Other cultural institutions of Czechs include musical organizations and theater groups. Czechs boast a rich heritage of music and drama dating from the Middle Ages. Amateur theater groups gained great popularity in Czech communities at the beginning of the 20th century. Chicago alone boasted six troupes of nonprofessional actors and one professional company, Ludvík's Theatrical Troupe. Born in Prague in 1842, František Ludvík pursued a career as an actor, traveling to the United States on tour in 1893. He loved the Windy City so much that he never returned home. His troupe enjoyed a great success among Chicago Czechs and performed regularly until Ludvík's death in 1910.

Throughout the Slavic world, ritual dramas connected with religious festivals have been popular for hundreds of years. For this reason Czech drama groups usually have been connected with either the Protestant or Catholic churches. Plays illustrating one aspect of a religious story, such as the Nativity, were commonly performed by young people.

Another popular subject for Czech drama lay in the rich tradition of Czech folklore, a wealth of stories and legends that have been a part of Czech culture for centuries. One of the most popular myths revolves around a 10th-century king named Wenceslas and his knights. According to Czech tradition these colorful figures

have never died but lie in wait in the mountains of Czechoslovakia, ready to awake when the time is right and fight a final, glorious battle. Another popular Czech folktale involves children who are born with their teeth and grow up into sorcerers, vampires, or witches. These stories are among the many Czech traditions carried to American shores and enjoyed by generations of Czech Americans across the United States.

*One way Czech Americans preserve their native culture is by dressing in traditional garments for holidays and festivals. These young women from Montgomery, Minnesota, struck a pose wearing the apparel of their ancestors in 1931.*

*Fast-food czar Ray Kroc stands in front of one of his many McDonald's restaurants during his tenure as chairman.*

# AN ERA OF EXCELLENCE

Since their arrival in the United States, Czech Americans have contributed to almost every field of endeavor in their new homeland. Although 19th-century Czech immigrants won acclaim as musicians, dramatists, journalists, politicians, and businessmen, they rarely received recognition outside the community of fellow Czechs. But the advent of the 20th century brought Czech Americans of achievement more fully into the public eye. By the 1970s, Czech names such as Cernan, Forman, Navratilova, and Serkin were recognizable to many Americans, not all of whom realized that these heroes belonged to a long tradition of Czech-American accomplishment.

## Ray Kroc

Thanks to one Czech American, millions of people across the United States daily enjoy a food more American than apple pie, the McDonald's hamburger. Ray Kroc, the founder of this fast-food empire, began his life in 1902 in American's greatest Czech enclave: Chicago, Illinois. As a teenager Kroc dreamed of becoming a musician. He departed from the classical piano taught him by his mother, a professional music teacher, and learned to play jazz, then a relatively new art form. Kroc found work with several orchestras but soon realized that he wanted to promote the music he loved, not play it. In 1922 he accepted a job as music director for WGES, a radio station in Chicago.

In 1929 the Jazz Age plummeted into the Great Depression, sending millions of Americans, including Kroc, to the brink of poverty. One winter he drove home to Chicago from a gig in a Florida nightclub, a journey he would long remember. In July 1968, he told *Nation's Business* magazine: "I was stone broke. I didn't have an overcoat, a topcoat, or a pair of gloves. When I got home I was frozen stiff, disillusioned and broke."

Kroc's luck soon changed for the better. He found employment with the Lily-Tulip Cup Company and soon worked his way up the corporate ladder to become the sales manager for the Midwest. His business brought him into contact with a new invention that changed his life, an electric mixer capable of concocting five milk shakes at once. Kroc left his sales post to found an independent company selling "multimixers." The blenders quickly became a familiar gadget at hamburger shops across the country—including the luncheonette of Mac and Dick McDonald.

In 1954, Kroc visited the McDonald brothers at their restaurant in San Bernadino, California, and discovered that they were earning a small fortune selling nothing but hamburgers, french fries, and milk shakes—created on one of eight multimixers. Kroc convinced the brothers to let him found a chain of drive-in hamburger restaurants identical to their own. Kroc even used the McDonald name and—as set forth in the original McDonald's contract—paid the brothers one-half of one percent of his gross profits.

On April 15, 1955, Kroc opened the first drive-in McDonald's in the Chicago suburb of Des Plaines. By the end of the year Kroc sold two franchises for the McDonald name and format, grossing hundreds of thousands of dollars. Within a few years he had made enough to buy out the McDonald brothers for $2,700,000—thus gaining exclusive rights to the McDonald name. By 1973, Kroc commanded a chain of 2,500 McDonald's restaurants, including those in such foreign cities as Paris and London. He served as chairman and then as senior chairman of the McDonald's board of directors.

Before his death in 1984, Kroc devoted time to other interests as well as McDonald's. For five years in the 1970s he owned the San Diego Padres baseball team. He also donated large gifts to his favorite charities, including the Ronald McDonald Houses, which provide housing for families of seriously ill children who are being treated at children's hospitals.

## Science and Mathematics

Astronaut Eugene Cernan, born in 1934, grew up in the Chicago suburb of Bellwood with his first-generation Czech-American parents. Cernan showed a fascination with planes from an early age. As a college student at Purdue University he joined the Navy ROTC program and set his sights on a career as a navy pilot.

After graduating with an engineering degree in 1956, Cernan began work as a navy jet pilot at the Naval Air Station at Miramar, California. He soon advanced to test pilot and entered a postgraduate program in aeronautical engineering. Even before finishing his master's degree, Cernan was admitted to the astronaut program at the National Aeronautics and Space Administration (NASA).

In 1964, Lieutenant Commander Cernan made his first trip into outer space, aboard the *Gemini 9*. He orbited the earth for three days, becoming the youngest astronaut ever to fly in space. Later, after aiding NASA on earth for several years, mostly as a test pilot of new space vehicles, Cernan participated in the *Apollo 10* mission in May 1969.

A few years later, in December 1972, Cernan took part in the *Apollo 17* mission, the program's last manned flight to the moon. He spent three days on the moon's surface, walking, driving a moon rover, and collecting rocks for scientific study. In March 1973, NASA awarded him a Bronze Eagle for his achievements in space.

The rockets that thrust Cernan into space owe much to the work of propulsion pioneer Frank Malina, de-

*Eugene Cernan sits for a portrait in his flight gear at NASA's Washington, D.C., headquarters.*

*Rocketeer and artist Frank Malina with a WAC Corporal missile, one of the weapons his pioneering studies made possible.*

scended from a Moravian father who had emigrated to Texas, where Frank was born in 1912. The family repatriated to the new republic of Czechoslovakia in 1920 but returned to the United States within five years so that Frank could reap the benefits of the American public school system.

Malina proved a talented student. He earned a bachelor of science degree in mechanical engineering from Texas A&M, and then a doctorate in aeronautics from the California Institute of Technology in 1940. During the next decade he designed America's first rocket-propelled missiles.

By the 1950s, Malina had switched careers and taken a position as head of the Division of Natural Sciences Research in the United Nations agency UNESCO. Two years later, he resigned to begin a third career, painting moveable three-dimensional objects. Eventually he became one of the foremost practitioners of kinetic art. In 1967 he founded *Leonardo: The International Journal of the Contemporary Artist.*

Rocketry and aeronautics are hardly the only area of science in which Czech Americans have made their mark. In 1947, Carl and Gerty Cori became the third married couple to share a Nobel Prize. They were honored for their research in the physiology of glucose (sugar) metabolism and the enzymes that control it.

Both Carl and Gerty were born in Prague; they met at medical school and married in 1920. Two years later, they joined the State Institute for the Study of Malignant Disease in Buffalo, New York. In 1931 they moved to Washington University in St. Louis, Missouri, where they performed their major research on glucose, glycogen, and insulin. (The metabolic pathways for glucose metabolism were named the Cori Cycle in their honor.) Gerty died in 1957. Carl remarried and continued teaching and research until his death in 1984.

In addition to science and technology, Czech immigrants to the New World have distinguished themselves in theoretical mathematics. One of the major theorems of 20th-century mathematics was discovered by Czech-born Kurt Gödel, who published his proof in 1931 while on the faculty of the University of Vienna in Austria. Gödel showed that any logical mathematical system must contain elements that cannot be proved or disproved using only the axioms of that system; therefore, mathematics itself can never be a closed, complete system. Gödel emigrated to the United States in 1940, and in 1953 he became a professor at the Institute for Advanced Study in Princeton, New Jersey, where he remained until his death in 1978.

## Music, Art, and Entertainment

Czech Americans have displayed a special talent for music. Rudolf Friml and Rudolf Serkin, both born in Bohemia, and Rudolf Firkusny, from Moravia, personify that rich musical tradition.

A native of Prague, Friml immigrated to the United States in 1906 at the age of 27. A composer as well as a pianist, he delighted American audiences with 33 light operas, especially *Firefly* (1912), *Rose Marie* (1924), and *The Vagabond King* (1925), which were produced both on stage and on film. Friml lived in the United States until his death in 1972.

Friml's compatriot Rudolf Serkin brought great delicacy to his interpretations of classical piano composi-

*During the late 1920s, Rudolf Friml spent a winter in the western Canadian town of Banff, composing a score for the play* The Squaw Man.

*Pianist Rudolf Serkin's renditions of classical compositions won him many admirers in the music world.*

tions. The son of Russian Jews, Serkin was born in Eger, Bohemia, in 1903. He spent his childhood in a single room with his parents and seven brothers and sisters. By the age of four he could both play the piano and read music. While still a child, he moved to Vienna to study with piano teacher Richard Robert, and he made his public debut with the Vienna Symphony at age 12.

Thereafter, Serkin shied away from public performances for several years. When he did begin to perform widely, he earned instant recognition in Europe. He made his American debut in the winter of 1936, soloing with the New York Philharmonic under Arturo Toscanini. In 1939 he became an American citizen and joined the staff of the Curtis Institute in Philadelphia, one of America's foremost conservatories, where he rose to the position of director in 1968. He also served as director of the Marlboro School of Music in Vermont.

Rudolf Serkin continued to perform until 1987. Though he died at his home in Vermont in 1991, his tradition lives on through his son, Peter, a pianist of almost as great renown as his father. Peter studied at the Curtis Institute beginning in 1958, at the age of 11, and debuted the next year at the Marlboro Festival. Since then he has performed with virtually every major orchestra and chamber group in the United States and Europe. He has taught on the faculties of the Curtis Institute, the Juilliard School, and the Tanglewood Music Center.

A contemporary of the elder Serkin, pianist Rudolf Firkusny was born in 1912 in Napajedla, Moravia. His particular interest lay in the repertoire of fellow Czech Leos Janaček, with whom he studied. Firkusny fled the German invasion of Czechoslovakia in 1939, settling in New York City. He performed throughout North and South America and Europe and also composed works for piano and string quartet.

Equally famous, and more controversial, was Andy Warhol, an American artist of Czech descent. He was born Andrew Warhola in Pittsburgh, Pennsylvania, in the late 1920s. By the 1960s, as a founder of the Pop Art movement, he became well known for his silk-screen paintings of comic-strip figures, popular personalities, and commercial designs—such as Campbell's soup cans.

He soon branched off into experimental films (including eight hours of a person sleeping), and he founded *Interview* magazine. In his New York studio known as "The Factory," he mass-produced silk-screen portraits of the famous. He died of somewhat mysterious causes in 1987.

Hollywood director Milos Forman is perhaps the most famous Czech American in the movies. His rise to the top of his profession is all the more remarkable considering that in 1940, at the age of eight, Forman lost both parents to Nazi concentration camps.

A native of Prague, Forman studied during the early 1950s at the Prague Film Faculty, where he developed an admiration for the works of Buster Keaton and Charlie Chaplin. In the 1960s, with such masterworks as *Loves of a Blonde*, he established Czechoslovakia as an important film center. In 1968 Forman found an international audience with *The Firemen's Ball*, which he envisioned as a political allegory. The film unfortunately outraged the firemen of Czechoslovakia, 40,000 of whom went on strike in protest.

In 1971 Forman moved to the United States to direct *Taking Off*, about a suburban American couple in

*Director Milos Forman (left) is interviewed while fans protest against his film* The People vs. Larry Flynt *at the 1997 Annual Academy Awards in Los Angeles. In spite of the film's controversial nature, Forman was nominated for Best Director.*

*Secretary of State Madeleine Albright gestures as she addresses government and international studies students during a 1998 forum on U.S. policy toward Iraq at the University of South Carolina in Columbia, S.C.*

search of their runaway hippie daughter. The Academy Award–winning success of *One Flew Over the Cuckoo's Nest* (1975) and *Amadeus* (1984) secured his reputation in Hollywood. Other Forman triumphs include *Hair* (1979), *Ragtime* (1981), and *The People vs. Larry Flynt* (1996).

Actress Sissy Spacek is a standout entertainer among Americans of Czech descent. Born in Quitman, Texas, Spacek caught attention with *Badlands* (1973), the story of a pair of serial killers. Since then, she has been nominated for Best Actress several times, and she won the Oscar in 1980 for *Coal Miner's Daughter*, a biography of country singer Loretta Lynn. Her other well-known films include *Carrie* (1976) and *Crimes of the Heart* (1986).

## Government and Diplomacy

As Secretary of State under President Bill Clinton, Madeleine Korbel Albright achieved the highest level of office of any woman in U.S. history. The daughter of a Czech diplomat, she fled the Nazis before World War II with her family, settling first in England, then in the United States.

At the outset of her political career, she served as a staff member for the National Security Council and as chief legislative assistant to Senator Edmund Muskie. In 1982, she joined the faculty of the Georgetown University School of Foreign Service, in Washington, D.C., as director of the Women in Foreign Service Program. She also served as director of the nonprofit Center for National Policy from 1988 to 1992.

In 1993 President Clinton appointed her U.S. Ambassador to the United Nations, a post she held until he named her Secretary of State in 1996. She became the first woman ever to head the State Department. Soon after her appointment, she discovered that, although she had been raised a Roman Catholic, her family was Jewish. Family members had hidden their affiliation to avoid the Nazi concentration camps, where three of her grandparents and other relatives died during World War II—a fate never revealed to her by her parents. She handled this revelation of her family's tragic past with grace and dignity.

The country that Albright's family fled had been established with the help of Louis Brandeis (1856–1941). He was born in Louisville, Kentucky, into a family whose roots in America traced back to Czech immigration in 1849. As a lawyer, Brandeis earned a reputation as the "people's attorney" by defending working-class people against large monopolies. In 1916, he became the first Jewish justice to serve on the United States Supreme Court. Two years later, he helped draft the Czechoslovakian Declaration of Independence.

## Sports

Born in Prague in 1956, tennis star Martina Navratilova inherited a legacy of tennis excellence from her grandmother, Agnes Semanski, who was ranked number two among Czech players before World War II. Navratilova's father coached her to three national women's championships by age 17.

As the top-ranked Czech woman, Navratilova was allowed to participate in a U.S. tour in 1973, during which she gained 20 pounds and failed to win any tournaments. In 1974, she joined the Virginia Slims circuit in the United States and defeated several highly ranked opponents but played erratically. But after a training regime at home, she defeated Margaret Court—one of the greatest players in the history of women's tennis—in the Australian Open in December 1974. One month later, she trounced both top-ranked Chris Evert and Virginia Wade.

Just as her professional career was taking off, however, she received a warning from the Czech government, which objected to her "Americanization." On September 6, 1975, Navratilova requested and received political asylum from the United States.

During the late 1970s and the 1980s, she reached the peak of her form, winning 18 Grand Slam titles, nine of them at Wimbledon—including six in a row (1982–87). She won 74 consecutive singles matches in 1984 and, with her partner Pam Shriver, an unrivaled 109 consecutive doubles matches (1983–85). Navratilova retired in 1994 with strong claim to being the greatest woman tennis player of all time.

*Tennis star Martina Navratilova hits a return shot to Monica Seles during a 1995 exhibition match in Atlantic City, N.J.*

Another Czech, Ivan Lendl, stands not far behind her in the tennis hierarchy. Ranked the world's top male player from 1985 to 1987, he ruled during a period of tough competition from the likes of Jimmy Connors, John McEnroe, and Bjorn Borg, collecting eight Grand Slam titles. He became a United States citizen in 1992 and retired from tennis in 1994—only to turn up on the golf circuit.

In hockey, Chicago Blackhawks star Stan Mikita, born in the Czech village of Sokolce, came to the United States as a child. In the 1960s he led the National Hockey League in scoring for four seasons, and he was awarded the Hart Trophy as the league's most valuable player in 1967 and 1968. His return home for a visit in 1968 became the subject of a documentary film, *Twenty-four Hours in Czechoslovakia*.

Among contemporary hockey stars is Bobby Holik, center for the New Jersey Devils, who won the 1995 Stanley Cup. Born in Jihlava, Czech Republic, in 1971, Holik became an American citizen in 1996. He is the nephew of Jiri Holik, one of the top goal-scorers in Czech history.

In baseball, the most famous Czech American is still Stan "the Man" Musial, a giant among major leaguers in the 1940s and early 1950s. Born in Donora, Pennsylvania, in 1920, he was National League batting champion seven times with the St. Louis Cardinals, and he was named the league's most valuable player in 1943, 1946, and 1948. With a career batting average of .331, he was elected to the Baseball Hall of Fame in 1969.

## Conclusion

In addition to the famous figures named in this chapter, many other Czech Americans have won distinction in business, politics, science, sports, and the arts. But even beyond their success in various careers, Czechs have contributed endlessly to the richness of American culture. Czech neighborhoods, founded on the outskirts of American cities, have merged all that is best about urban and rural living. The Czech commitment to education has produced a community of highly informed citizens who bring their insight and awareness to bear on every facet of American life. Czech Americans can regard their manifold achievements with pride, for the Czech tradition represents one of the most vibrant threads in the American tapestry.

# FURTHER READING

Bernardo, Stephanie. *The Ethnic Almanac*. New York: Doubleday, 1981.

Cather, Willa. *My Ántonia*. Boston: Houghton Mifflin, 1918.

Galens, Judy, Anna Sheets, and Robyn V. Young, eds. *Gale Encyclopedia of Multicultural America*, Vol. 1. Detroit: Gale Research, 1995.

Hamsik, Dusan. *Writers Against Rulers*. London: Hutchinson, 1971.

Keefe, Eugene, et al. *Area Handbook for Czechoslovakia*. Washington, DC: Foreign Area Studies, 1972.

Laska, Vera, ed. *The Czechs in America, 1633–1977: A Chronology and Fact Book*. Dobbs Ferry, NY: Oceana, 1978.

Masaryk, Tomáš G. *The Meaning of Czech History*. Chapel Hill: University of North Carolina Press, 1974.

Roucek, Joseph S. *The Czechs and Slovaks in America*. Minneapolis, MN: Lerner Publications, 1967.

# INDEX

Albright, Madeleine Korbel, 104
Allies, 31, 35
American Revolution, 42, 44–45
Apostles to the Slavs, 19
Austria, 29, 30
Austro-Hungarian Empire, 30–31

Benedictines' College of St.
    Procopius, 78
Beneš, Edvard, 22, 34–36
Bergman, Ernst, 55
Bohemia, 13, 17, 19, 20, 29, 34,
    47–48
Bohemia, Long Island, 82–83
Bohemia Manor, 41
Bohemia River, 41
Boihemum, 18
Brandeis, Louis, 105
Budweiser beer, 54

Caledonia, Wisconsin, 52
Čapek, Tomas, 61, 88
Cather, Willa, 75
Catholic Central Union, 91
Catholicism, 19, 22, 24, 25, 85–87
Catholic Union of Texas, 92
Čechs in America, The (Čapek), 61,
    64
Central Powers, 31
Čermák, Anton, 77
Cernan, Eugene, 99
Charles I, 20
Charles IV, 20, 26
Charles VI, 26
Charles University, 20, 28
Charter 77, 37
Chicago, Illinois, 13, 52, 56, 79–81,
    94
Civic Forum, 37
Cleveland Agreement (1915), 30, 32

Comenius (Komenský, Jan Ámos),
    43
Communism, 34–37
Cori, Carl and Gerty, 101
Cyril, 19
Czech Americans
    areas settled by, 13–14, 42, 43, 45,
        52, 54–55, 73, 79–83
    in business, 41, 54, 98–99
    community life of, 13
    education and, 43, 45, 78–79
    as factory workers, 62–64
    famous Czech Americans,
        98–106
    farmland settlements, 52–54, 64,
        73–74
    folkways, 94–95
    fraternal and benevolent societies,
        90–93
    as immigrants, 13, 39, 42, 47–51,
        55–56, 58–59
    journey to United States, 50
    music and dance of, 74–76,
        101–102
    musicians, 101–102
    newspapers of, 87–90
    politics and politicians, 76–78,
        93
    preservation of heritage, 14–15
    reasons for immigration, 39, 41
        47–49, 56, 58–59
    religion and, 85–87
    scientists, 99–101
    size of population, 14
    sokols and, 14, 93–94
    suburban settlements, 56–57,
        82–83
    theater and drama and, 94–95,
        102–103
    traditional culture of, 75–76
Czechoslovak Christian
    Democracy, 93

Czechoslovakia
  communism in, 34–37
  formation of, 17
Czechoslovak National Council of
  America, 92–93
Czecho-Slovak Protective Society, 83
Czechoslovak Society of America, 92
Czech Republic, history of, 17–37
Czech-Slavonic Benevolent Society
  (CSPS), 90–91

Debs, Eugene V., 78
*Dělnické listy*, 89
Dobrovský, Josef, 26
Dual Monarchy, 29
Dubček, Alexander, 37
Dvořák, Antonín, 74
Dvornik, Francis, 50

Ellis Island, 51
England, 34

Ferdinand I, 24
Ferdinand II, 25
Ferdinand III, 26
Firkusny, Rudolf, 102
Forman, Milos, 103–104
Freethinkers movement, 87, 89, 90,
  93
Friml, Rudolf, 101

Georgia, 42
Germany, 32–35, 47
Gödel, Kurt, 101
Golden Bull, 20
Gorbachev, Mikhail, 37
Gottwald, Klement, 36
Great Moravia, 18, 19–20

Hácha, Emil, 33
Hack, George, 40
Haidusek, Augustin, 76–77
Hapsburg Empire, 13, 24–29, 85–86
Havel, Václav, 37

Herman, Augustine, 39–41
Hitler, Adolf, 32–33, 35
*Hlas*, 89
Holik, Bobby, 106
Homestead Act (1862), 52
Hungary, 19, 29, 30, 33
Hus, Jan, 20–21, 83
Husák, Gustáv, 37
Hussite movement, 21–22
Hussite Wars, 21–23, 27

Illinois, 14, 51, 54. *See also* Chicago,
  Illinois

Jakes, Milos, 37
Jan Hus Presbyterian Church, 86
Johnson-Reed Act (1924), 57
Jonáš, Charles, 89–90
Joseph I, 26
Jungman, Josef, 26–27

*Katolické Noviny*, 89
*Katolík*, 89
Klaus, Václav, 37
Komenský, Jan Ámos, 43
Kroc, Ray, 97–99

Lendl, Ivan, 106
Leopold I, 26
Libuše, Queen, 18–19
Lidice, Czechoslovakia, 35
Litomysy, Minnesota, 14
Ludvík, František, 94
Ludvík's Theatrical Troupe, 94
Luther, Martin, 23

Malina, Frank, 99–100
Maria Theresa, 26–27
Masaryk, Jan, 36
Masaryk, Tomáš Garrigue, 31–32
McDonalds, 97–99
Meilbek, Leo, 78
Methodius, 19
Mikita, Stan, 106
Milligan, Nebraska, 14, 52, 81–82

Moravia, 13, 17, 20, 34
Moravian Bretheren, 41–45, 87
Moravian College, 43
Moravian Trombone Choir, 45
Munich Pact, 33
Musial, Stan, 106
*My Ántonia* (Cather), 75


*Národ*, 89
*Národní Noviny*, 89
National Czech and Slovak
    Museum and Library, 83
Nationalism, 27–30
National origins plan, 57–58
National Sokol Union, 94
Native Americans, 45
Navratilova, Martina, 105
Nebraska, 54
Neumann, Jan Nepomuk, 47
New Prague, Minnesota, 14
New York, 13, 50, 52, 54, 56
North Carolina, 42, 45
*Noviny Lípy Slovanské*, 49


Ohio, 54
Otakar I, King, 20
Otto I, 20


Palacký, František, 26–27
Pennsylvania, 41–43, 45
Pilsen, Iowa, 14
Pilsen beer, 54
Pittsburgh Agreement (1918),
    30–31, 32
*Pokrok*, 89
Poland, 33
Potsdam Conference (1945), 36
Prague Spring, 37
*Pravda Vítezí*, 22
Přemyslid rulers, 19, 20
Presbyterians, 86, 87
Protestantism, 24–25, 86–87
Protestant Reformation, 23–24
Public Against Violence, 37

Republic of Czechoslovakia, 32
Roman Empire, 17–18, 19–20
Rosewater, Edgar, 77


Sabath, Adolph, 77
St. Jan Nepomuk, 87
Serkin, Rudolf, 101–102
Sigismund, 21, 22–23
Silesia, 17
*Slavie*, 89–90
Slovakia, 17, 18, 20, 37
Slovak People's party, 32
Slovaks, 30–34
*Slován Amerikanskáy*, 89
Socialist Labor party, 77–78
*Sokols*, 14, 93–94
Soviet Union, 35, 37
Spacek, Sissy, 104
*Spravedlnost*, 89
Stalin, Joseph, 35–37
Sudetenland, 32–33


Texas, 14, 50, 55, 73, 76
Thirty Years' War, 24–26, 42
Tyrs, Miroslav, 93


Union of Czech Women, 92


Velvet Revolution, 37


Warhol, Andy, 102–103
Wenceslaus, King, 94–95
Whitefield, George, 42
White Mountain, Battle of, 25, 39,
    43
Wilson, Woodrow, 32
Wisconsin, 54
World War I, 30–32
World War II, 34–35


Zirovnice, Czechoslovakia, 64
Žižka, Jan, 22
Zvolánek, Joseph, 55

STEPHANIE SAKSON-FORD received an M.A. in philosophy from the University of Hawaii and edits American history, among other topics, for a New York–based publisher. Her grandfather was from Czechoslovakia.

DANIEL PATRICK MOYNIHAN is the senior United States senator from New York. He is also the only person in American history to serve in the cabinets or subcabinets of four successive presidents—Kennedy, Johnson, Nixon, and Ford. Formerly a professor of government at Harvard University, he has written and edited many books, including *Beyond the Melting Pot*, *Ethnicity: Theory and Experience* (both with Nathan Glazer), *Loyalties*, and *Family and Nation*.

# PICTURE CREDITS